The Legends of Manchester City

The Legends of Manchester City

IAN PENNEY

breedon **books**
PUBLISHING

First published in Great Britain in 2002 by
The Breedon Books Publishing Company
Limited
Breedon House, 3 The Parker Centre,
Derby, DE21 4SZ.

ISBN 1 85983 326 8

Printed and bound by Butler & Tanner, Frome,
Somerset, England.

Cover printing by Lawrence-Allen Colour
Printers, Weston-super-Mare, Somerset.

Contents

This book is dedicated
to Lonnie Yates.
A true friend and one
who will be missed.

Introduction

LEGENDS, aka folklore, myths and tradition.

Or in footballing terms, players that played for your team over a substantial period, cheered up many a wintery afternoon of your youth and who now reflect warmly in the autumn of your mind; people who the fans regularly looked forward to seeing play and were disappointed when their favourite names were scrubbed out of the programme with a bright yellow, school issue biro. Entertainers, goalscorers (and goalkeepers), creative midfielders and solid, rock-like defenders, each kind of player different in his own way and yet a personal favourite of thousands. Any newcomer having the audacity to replace one of these 'legends' had a huge task to perform even before a ball was kicked.

People, sadly some no longer with us, who made ordinary, run-of-the-mill football clubs into world-famous names.

Hopefully this book captures the essence of some 100 of these people connected with Manchester City, although some entries included herein had no impact whatsoever on the 90 minutes of kicking a ball about once or twice a week. For all that, though, their efforts behind the scenes warrant inclusion at the expense of some much more vaunted players, many of whom wore the shirt and promised plenty, but unfortunately delivered a lot less. Each and every one of this personal selection of 100 names has contributed hugely to the successes and history of Manchester City.

Some will obviously be much better known than others. Some, of course, will be of a much more recent vintage than others. Some will undoubtedly cause discussion along the lines of, "What's he included him for?" whilst missing entries will no doubt raise the inevitable, "Why isn't he in?"

Apart from one season, Manchester City Football Club has played more than 100 years in the top two divisions of English football, collecting championships, cups and a European prize along the way. As the club continues into its third century (as reigning First Division champions) a move from its spiritual home in Moss Side is a little over 12 months away. Hopefully the club's new home will provide as many, if not more, great games, great players and great entertainment for its remarkably loyal army of supporters.

When I was asked by Breedon Books to write this book, it seemed the ideal moment to recollect the great names of the past as the club was about to embark into an exciting new era.

Hopefully it will bring back some happy memories for fans who saw their heroes play and will provide an insight into the days of Meredith and Furness, the days before the wireless let alone interactive cable television.

If fans don't like the text, at least they'll have a beautifully produced autograph book and with it, an ideal way to record a piece of Manchester City's history.

Ian Penney
July 2002

Malcolm Allison – a man ahead of his time

WHEN Malcolm Allison received a 'phone call and job offer from Joe Mercer in the summer of 1965, no one could have realised the amazing success they would bring to Manchester City. With Mercer's calmness at the helm and Allison's brilliant coaching abilities, the two embarked on the greatest period ever in the club's history.

In his younger days Allison had been a useful centre-half and had joined Charlton Athletic as an 18-year-old in 1945. Six years later he moved to West Ham United where, like many of his playing contemporaries at Upton Park, he developed a passion for all aspects of tactics and coaching. His playing career ended at Sheffield one day in 1958 when, in his own words, "Their guy just ran away from me. I had no breath left to catch him." The 31-year-old Allison had developed tuberculosis; a disease that cost him a lung and forced him to spend 12 months in a sanatorium.

Still fascinated by the game, Allison continued with his courses at Lilleshall and was given a chance to get back into football at non-League Bath City, a side, which at the time contained another future City legend, full-back Tony Book. He had also had spells with Cambridge University and Toronto before being offered his first League job at Plymouth Argyle. Although no one doubted his obvious ability, many branded Allison a big-mouth and a man who had yet to prove himself on the big stage. The 'phone call from Mercer finally gave him that opportunity. With Allison having this reputation and Mercer himself recently the victim of a severe illness, both men possibly had points to prove and an ailing football club in Moss Side gave them ample opportunity.

Allison inherited several 'ordinary' players such as Mike Doyle, Alan Oakes, Glyn Pardoe and Neil Young on his arrival at Maine Road. Within 12 months City were Second Division champions and these players were becoming well-known the length and breadth of the country as the nucleus of a team that was certainly going places. When Mike Summerbee, Colin Bell, Francis Lee and Tony Book arrived over the next two years, City had indeed gone places; they were now First Division champions and were playing for the first time in Europe. Allison was right when he said City would terrify Europe; the only thing was he had to wait nearly two years for his prediction to come true. Well he has always said he was ahead of his time!

Not only were City a team of exceptionally skilled footballers, they were also – by a long way – the fittest side in the country. A large credit for City's success in the late 1960s and early 1970s must go to Allison, not only for his expert guidance in the way he got so much from his players, but also for his training methods which were years ahead of anything else currently in use.

Not surprisingly, after all the years of success, Allison wanted the title of team manager. In 1971, when Joe Mercer firstly moved 'upstairs' and then later on to Coventry City, Allison was given total control of team affairs. It was possibly the beginning of his undoing. As a coach, quite simply there was no one better anywhere; managing the side though was different. Together Joe Mercer and Malcolm Allison made Manchester City; they never missed a trick. By their own admittances, neither of them could have done the job on their own.

In 1973 he left Maine Road after less than a full season in charge and moved to Crystal Palace although it was not the last time Manchester City would see Big Mal. After a second spell with Plymouth and then spending time in Turkey and the United States he returned in July 1979, initially as number two to former captain and now manager Tony Book. Perhaps not too surprisingly, Allison's larger than life personality gradually overshadowed his former player and before long it was plain to see who was making the decisions. Unfortunately, however forward thinking these decisions might have been, they still appear as strange today as they did all those years back. His much-publicised 'clear-out' of established stars such as Gary Owen and Peter Barnes ultimately cost both Book and Allison their jobs in October 1980.

Allison then found himself returning to Crystal Palace for a while before setting off once again on his travels, taking in such places as Kuwait and Portugal, finally settling in Yarm just outside Middlesbrough (where he spent 18 months as manager) in the early 1980s. In later years Allison has kept in touch with the game by doing some part-time scouting work for Arsenal.

As the new century arrived, Allison – by now in his 70s – suffered both personal and medical problems and returned to Manchester where some of his former players – not least Mike Summerbee and Francis Lee – tried their utmost to help out their former mentor. Despite all his problems Allison still has strong affections for Manchester City (as indeed do City fans from that era have of him) and was a regular at home games during the Blues' successful First Division campaign last season.

Sam Barkas – full-back for City, inside-right for England

SAM Barkas held a unique collection of Football League championship medals. In 1929 he won a Third Division North one with his first club Bradford City, followed by a First Division one in 1936-37 and then a Second Division one 10 years later; the last two were won in the colours of Manchester City.

Born in South Shields on 29 December 1909, Barkas was one of four brothers who all played League football. Like his medal collection, is this another record? He joined City from Bradford in April 1934 for a fee reported to be in the region of £5,000 and just in time to play in the last two League games of the season. His debut came in a 3-2 defeat at Anfield on 2 May; a game played four days after City had beaten Portsmouth in the FA Cup Final. He played in all bar one League game the following season, scoring just once, ironically on the opening day at West Bromwich Albion. It turned out to be his one and only goal for the Blues.

Without doubt Barkas had joined a very successful City side and over the next four seasons his was one of the first names penciled in on the team sheet. A cultured left-back in the days when the norm was to just to clear the lines, Barkas won five England caps during his time at Maine Road, a figure that would undoubtedly have been more had it not been for the apparently never-ending presence of Arsenal's Eddie Hapgood. In England's 5-1 win over Ireland in Belfast in 1937, Barkas, at left-back, partnered another City full-back in Bert Sproston. Such was his ability with the ball that against Belgium in 1936 (his debut for England) he played at inside-right in the 3-2 defeat.

Like many other players of his era, the outbreak of World War Two robbed Barkas of arguably his best years. He returned to Wilf Wild's side as a 35-year-old in August 1945 and played 33 games in what was at the time, the Football League North. In January 1946 he had the misfortune to be in a Blues' side that lost 8-2 to Bradford City at Maine Road in a fourth-round FA Cup tie, a result that is still City's biggest home defeat of all time. Normal Football League status returned the following season with Barkas now installed as captain and City continuing where they'd left off some six years before, namely in Division Two. Coincidentally he played exactly the same number of League games that term as well, 33, with the final one a convincing 5-1 win against Newport County, a game that saw City crowned as Second Division champions for the fifth time. It was also Roy Clarke's first appearance in City's colours.

In May 1947, Barkas decided to take over as manager of non-League Workington Town instead of leading City into Division One but it wasn't the end of his connection with Maine Road. After a brief spell working with Wigan Athletic he returned in 1957 at the request of then manager Les McDowall to take up scouting duties for the Blues. Leaving Maine Road for a second time, Barkas later became a scout with Leeds United before finishing his football connections coincidentally with the club he'd started them, Bradford City, when he was employed by their commercial department to supervise their pools' scheme. Barkas stayed behind the scenes with Bradford until his retirement in November 1964. He passed away at his home in Shipley on 8 December 1989, just three weeks before his 80th birthday.

Maine Road career

195 games   1 goal

Horace Barnes – forever in the record books

ALTHOUGH the name Horace Barnes may not be known to some of today's younger supporters, he will always hold a unique place in the history of Manchester City Football Club. He scored City's first-ever goal at Maine Road. That goal against Sheffield United in August 1923 came more than nine years after he'd joined the Blues from Derby County.

Born in the small village of Wadsley Bridge (ironically near Sheffield, a town where he played his early football in the Sunday School League), Barnes arrived at Hyde Road shortly before the last full season prior to the outbreak of World War One. His fee of £2,500 was reported as being the highest authenticated fee up to that time. Standing just short of 5ft 8in tall and weighing $11\frac{1}{2}$st, Barnes was a strongly-built inside-left who came to City with a reputation of being a prolific goalscorer, one that had been built up during the best part of six years with Derby. It was with Derby that he won his one and only competitive honour; a Second Division championship medal in 1912.

He scored on his debut on the opening day of the 1914-15 season in a 4-1 home win against Bradford City and played a further 28 League and Cup games that term adding another 13 goals. He'd started a career with City that would average a goal in every other game for the next 10 years.

He bettered that remarkable feat in the wartime competitions. Until normal soccer was resumed at the end of August 1919, Barnes played in 73 wartime games for the Blues and scored an incredible 73 goals. He is also reported to have wanted to play for City so much in a game against Stockport County in 1915 that he left his work unauthorised from a munitions factory and was fined by Manchester magistrates for his trouble.

It seemed as though 'official' or 'unofficial' games made no difference to him. On the normal League resumption, Barnes scored twice in a 3-3 draw against, of all teams, Sheffield United. Along with Tommy Browell (another player who averaged a goal every other game) Barnes formed a formidable scoring partnership and had a reputation for being a fierce striker of the ball particularly with his left foot. Despite his obvious goalscoring abilities, his one and only England appearance came in a Victory International against Wales in Cardiff in October 1919, although he did make two other appearances for the Football League.

On 27 March 1920 City beat Liverpool 2-1 in front of a crowd close to 40,000 at Hyde Road. The players were introduced on the pitch before the game to His Royal Highness King George V who was on a tour of the North-west at the time. By all accounts the King stayed for the whole game and enjoyed his visit. Never one to be outdone by anyone when it came to football, Barnes scored both City's goals that day.

In November 1924, the 34-year-old Barnes was sold to Preston North End for £2,750, a fine piece of business by manager David Ashworth as it meant City were £250 in profit on Barnes' career. He stayed at Deepdale for 12 months before being transferred to Oldham Athletic until retiring from the Football League in his 37th year. Even if the years had caught him up, Horace Barnes had certainly not forgotten how to score goals. Playing for non-League Ashton National, he managed to score 80 times during the 1928-29 season, and then scored six in just 30 minutes playing for the Rest of Cheshire in a game against Port Vale.

His level of fitness built up over many years as professional footballer ensured Barnes could continue his employment at an east Manchester engineering firm until he was 70. Tragically he was to have a short retirement; he passed away at his home in Clayton on 12 September 1961, less than a year after his retirement.

Only six players have ever scored more League goals for City than Horace Barnes, his achievements remembered by a street close to Maine Road being named after him in 1977.

Hyde Road-Maine Road career

235 appearances   125 goals

Ken Barnes – "best uncapped wing-half in the country"

THE quote about Ken Barnes at the top of this page comes from no lesser player – and not too bad a judge of a footballer – than Denis Law. Law was a young up and coming player at Maine Road in 1960 when Barnes was captain at the club and the free-scoring Scotsman listened to his skipper's advice off the field as well as on it for it was Barnes who first taught Law how to drive.

Born the proverbial stone's throw from Birmingham ground at St Andrew's in March 1929, Barnes turned out regularly for their colts' side but it was whilst serving as an aircraftsman with the RAF that professional clubs began to show an interest. Bolton Wanderers were very keen to sign him but he surprised everyone when he signed for non-League Stafford Rangers (a club he'd played for on occasion whilst with the RAF) when his demob came. Barnes' reason for this was quite simple; "I just liked it there," he said years later.

At Stafford other clubs began to look at this lean, strong-running and creative right-half with a view to giving him the chance to show off his skills at a higher level. His hometown side Birmingham were one, as were neighbours West Bromwich Albion along with Sheffield Wednesday and Manchester City. Fortunately he chose Maine Road, signing in May 1950 for the princely sum of £900.

His introduction to the first team was a slow one; he played just one senior game in his first four years at the club, a 4-2 home win against Derby County in January 1952. However, his time spent in the reserves had not been wasted. Along with centre-forward Johnny Williamson, Barnes began to develop a style of play not too dissimilar from the one used by the brilliant Hungarian national side of the time. Put simply, this involved the traditional centre-forward playing a lot deeper than was the norm for the day; the idea being that if the opposition centre-half went with him then gaps aplenty would open up at the back. Barnes used his considerable passing skills to full effect as the Blues' second team went on a run of more than 20 games without defeat. The next step was to try this method in the first team.

At first manager Les McDowall was a bit sceptical about the idea but was finally persuaded by amongst others, Williamson and trainer and former player Fred Tilson. It was not an unqualified success. It was the first game of the 1954-55 season and City lost 5-0 at Preston North End. On paper at least the plan was sound but one key element was missing; Ken Barnes was still in the reserves. The general consensus of opinion was that in order to make the plan work properly, Barnes would need to be given a run in the first team. Three days after the Preston defeat City played Sheffield United at Maine Road. Barnes was in a City side that won 5-2. With 'Beaky' linking up well with Revie, the plan worked beautifully; he played in all bar one of the remaining League games that season and when May came around City were lining up at Wembley to play Newcastle United in the FA Cup Final. Unfortunately after going a goal down in the first minute and then having full-back Jimmy Meadows carried off with a knee injury, 10 men City tried their best but lost 3-1.

12 months later though City, having stuck with the style of play that had been christened the Revie Plan, were back at Wembley. This time though (and despite Bert Trautmann breaking his neck) they managed to come away victorious, beating Birmingham by the same scoreline they'd lost to Newcastle by.

In the latter half of the 1950s Barnes became a vital member of City's side as well as the regular penalty taker and captain. In December 1957 he wrote his name in City's record books when he scored a hat-trick of penalties in a 6-2 win against Everton. For all his skill and ability (both recognised not only at Maine Road) Barnes failed to get full recognition by England. The nearest he came to international honours was when he was named as a reserve against Wales in 1957 although he did turn out for the Football League.

On 4 May 1961 Barnes left City to become player-manager at Wrexham, a position he later held at Witton Albion. In 1970 he resigned as manager of Bangor City to return to Maine Road as trainer-coach, one of many backroom positions he was to hold over the next 22 years.

In 1992 – after seeing his son Peter play for both City and England – Barnes was granted a testimonial game against Manchester United and retired from 'active service'. Now in his 70s, one of the club's greatest practical jokers (and heaviest smokers!) is still a regular visitor to the ground as well as being an active member of the club's Former Players' Association.

Maine Road career

283 appearances   19 goals

Peter Barnes – the one that got away

ALWAYS a great advocate of skill in the game, Peter Barnes certainly lived up to his beliefs as he became one of the most exciting and skilful players ever on City's books.

The son of former 1950s favourite Ken, Peter had impressed enough during his schoolboy footballing days to be offered an apprenticeship at Maine Road as a 15-year-old in 1972. Two years later he'd turned professional and his first senior appearance came as a substitute for Glyn Pardoe in an unfortunate fourth-round League Cup defeat at Old Trafford in October 1974. Manager Tony Book seemed suitably impressed with the young winger that just three days later – at Burnley in a League game – Barnes found himself starting a senior game for the first time. He played in just three games of his debut season but for the next four years he was an integral part of a fine City side that was always on the lookout for goals.

With Dennis Tueart on the left and Joe Royle and Brian Kidd in the middle, Barnes operated primarily on the right, a position giving him ample opportunity to cut inside and score some memorable goals with his more favoured left foot. Having said that though on many occasions Barnes and Tueart would change sides and it became a common sight in the mid-1970s to see opposition defences frantically back-pedalling as wave after wave of rampaging City attacks converged on them.

By the time the 1976 League Cup Final came around Barnes was a first-team regular. He also managed to score the first goal at Wembley as City beat Newcastle United 2-1, a goal and a victory that pre-empted by just 24 hours him being confirmed as the PFA Young Player of the Year. The following November, Barnes made his England debut in a 2-0 World Cup qualifier against Italy at Wembley. On top of his eight England Youth caps and his nine Under-21s, it was the first of 14 full caps he'd win whilst at Maine Road. Only five players have played more for England during their time with City. By the time he'd finished playing in 1988, Barnes had gone on to win 22 caps for his country.

In July 1979, Barnes had played over 120 times for the Blues' first team, was still only 22 and looked set to become a permanent fixture in the side for many years to come. Unfortunately for him (and, with hindsight Manchester City) Malcolm Allison had returned and had his own plans. Along with his good friend Gary Owen, Barnes didn't feature in these plans and the couple soon found themselves on their way to West Bromwich Albion. It was a bitter pill for both players and fans to swallow. To make things worse when West Bromwich travelled to Maine Road for a League game the following February they won 3-1 with Barnes scoring twice as if to rub salt in the wounds.

After 23 goals in 76 League games in a two-year spell, Barnes left The Hawthorns and moved to Leeds United for two seasons. The next six years saw him ply his trade at a whole range of clubs ranging from Spanish side Real Betis, through to Coventry City and neighbours Manchester United. For all his travels though Barnes was (and still is) an out and out Blue and when Jimmy Frizzell offered him the chance to come home in January 1987 he leapt at it. Regrettably though his second spell was not as successful as his first. Dogged by a series of niggling injuries, Barnes could only manage a further eight first-team games before loan periods with Bolton Wanderers and Port Vale.

In later years Barnes turned out for Hull City, Sunderland (albeit just once), Portuguese side Farense and (many times) for City's Old Boys team. After a brief flirtation with management at non-League Runcorn he returned once again to Maine Road, passing on his experience and knowledge to the footballers of tomorrow at the Platt Lane training academy. At the time of writing he is City's match summariser for a local radio station and makes regular appearances at Supporters' Club meetings.

Peter Barnes had a playing career that spanned nearly 20 years and 20 clubs. Many felt that the best and largest part of that time should have been spent with just the one.

Maine Road career

149-12 appearances   22 goals

Colin Bell – the most complete City player

QUITE simply, Colin Bell was a magnificent footballer. Passing, shooting, heading, scoring, in fact all aspects of the game seemed to come naturally to a player many think is the greatest ever to wear the famous sky blue shirt. When all his football ability is added to his tremendous stamina, it's hard to disagree with that statement. In fact some experienced athletes actually said if he hadn't been such a good footballer he could have easily made the grade as a top-flight middle distance runner.

Bell joined Bury as a 17-year-old in 1963 and ironically made his debut in League football against City (and scored) in a 1-1 draw the following year. By March 1966 he had already proved to be one of the Second Division's best young prospects and was attracting scouts from most of the country's top sides. One person certainly interested was City's Malcolm Allison, a man always vociferous with his opinions, only this time they were very negative. So determined was Allison to get Bell to Maine Road he would spend hours criticising him in front of other interested parties in the hope they'd be put off. In the end it worked; Bell signed for City on 16 March for £45,000. His debut came three days later in a 2-1 win at Derby County when he also managed to score, although even he would admit that Ron Webster's clearance striking him in the small of the back and then rebounding into the net was not one of his greatest goals.

Less than two months after signing, Bell was joining in the celebrations with his new teammates as City were crowned champions of the Second Division. It was the first of five pieces of silverware in a glorious five-year period.

Although primarily a midfield player, Bell was more than capable of scoring the odd goal, indeed only two players have scored more for City in the club's history.

During the Mercer-Allison years Bell was not only arguably the key player for City but he also established himself in the England set-up. He made his debut for the national side against Sweden in May 1968, less than two weeks after City's First Division triumph at Newcastle. It was the first of 48 caps, still a club record for any country, and he was on the losing side in just eight of those games. Along with Francis Lee, he was part of Alf Ramsey's party for the Mexico World Cup of 1970, replacing Bobby Charlton in the ill-fated defeat by West Germany.

Bell continued to turn in consistently high performances for both club and country throughout the early 1970s and was recognised and liked by supporters of other teams for simply being the outstanding player he was.

In November 1975, still only 29, Bell suffered a horrific knee injury that effectively curtailed a playing career many thought, because of his extraordinary high level of fitness, could have gone on for at least another six years. During the 4-0 League Cup victory against Manchester United, he was the victim of a mistimed tackle by Martin Buchan and was stretchered off. He managed to make a further four League appearances that season but would then be out of first-team action until Boxing Day 1977.

His return (as a substitute against Newcastle in a 4-0 win – it was 0-0 when he came on at the start of the second-half) lifted the team and began a run of seven straight wins. For anyone connected with the club if was marvellous to once again see 'Nijinksky' in action.

However, it would not last. His injury had proved so serious that no matter how hard he and the medical staff tried, the 'old' Colin Bell had unfortunately gone. He played in 17 games (including two as substitute) of the 1978-79 season before finally being forced to retire on 21 August. The last of his 153 goals for the club was against FC Twente Enschede in a UEFA Cup tie.

Eleven years after his enforced and premature retirement, Bell returned to the Maine Road and joined the coaching staff working particularly with the young players. Nowadays (still looking remarkably fit) he is employed by the club's corporate division and as such can be seen at most home games.

As far as television coverage is concerned, Colin Bell played in the wrong era; in 2002 his talents would be known the world over. It's very hard to tell the younger supporters just how good he was; seeing is believing. Those supporters of a more senior vintage – and indeed those who played with and against him – will never forget just what a talent he was. When Malcolm Allison says he was the best player he ever worked with, you know he must have been a bit special.

Maine Road career
498-3 appearances   153 goals

Ali Benarbia – The best free transfer ever?

WITHOUT wishing to insult the intelligence of Manchester City supporters everywhere, it's probably fair to say that prior to the start of the 2001-02 season, not many of them had heard the name Ali Benarbia. By the end of it, everybody knew who he was and the best part of 30,000 people chanted it (well at least the first part) at every home game.

Some might say the fact that he's only played one season at Maine Road hardly qualifies him for legendary status. For every one that says that (surely they can't have seen him play) there must be at least five who'll disagree.

He was arguably the best player in City's successful First Division championship campaign in his first season with the club. The fact that the team equalled its all-time League goalscoring record of 108 in that season (a record since 1926-27) was due in no small part to the skill and vision of this diminutive Algerian midfielder. A wonderful passer with the canny knack of knowing exactly the right moment to play the ball through opposition's defences (sometimes with a backheel no less), Benarbia set up countless chances for the forwards, especially Shaun Goater and Darren Huckerby who netted 48 times between them.

He arrived at Maine Road in September 2001, amazingly on a free transfer from top French side Paris St Germain where he'd been captain. Fortunately for Manchester City, manager Kevin Keegan was more than aware of the talent the 32-year-old Benarbia could bring to his resurgent team and gave him his debut in English football in a 3-0 home win against Birmingham. Not renowned as a goalscorer, he then promptly scored in each of his next three League games. His arrival in Manchester coincided with the return from injury of another skilful midfielder Eyal Berkovic, and many thought it would not be possible to play them both in the same side because of their similarities. Keegan though didn't think it would be a problem and so it proved as the pair of them literally carved up defences week after week. Of the two players, Benarbia appears to be the most capable of 'handling himself', a fact proved when he had a front tooth completely knocked out against Crystal Palace and then proceeded to get up and flash a huge toothless grin at the Kippax Stand before continuing the game.

Benarbia had played all his football prior to City in France, a country his family had emigrated to when he was just a two-year-old. Before Paris St Germain, he'd been with Monaco (where he won the French championship and played in a side that knocked Manchester United out of the Champions League) and later Bordeaux where he won the French Player of the Year award. Qualified by residence to play for France, his talents have been curiously overlooked by their national side, a point that eventually persuaded him to play for the country of his birth. To date he has three caps for Algeria although it does seem a pity that his flair and aptitude appear destined not to be seen on a world stage.

Not only is Benarbia a joy to watch, he also provides no shortage of guidance and encouragement to many of his teammates with the young Shaun Wright-Phillips in particular seemingly improving each week playing alongside him.

With Goater and Huckerby's goals, the consistently high performances of Kevin Horlock and Richard Dunne and the emergence of the aforementioned Wright-Phillips, the Player of the Season vote for the wonderful 2001-02 season was always going to be a close one. In the end it went to Benarbia; it was a hugely popular choice. It also confirmed that there is still room in the English game for the more skilful player, in other words the kind that's always welcome at Maine Road.

He was presented with his award on the pitch after the final game of the season, a 3-1 home win against Portsmouth. Minutes before this he'd also had his hands on the First Division championship trophy, the culmination of a fabulous first year's work for his new club. Carrying the famous old trophy around the pitch, Benarbia had a huge, ear-to-ear, grin on his face and his enjoyment was there for all to see. There was no questioning the fact that he loves playing for City as much as its fans love watching him.

Maine Road career

42 appearances   8 goals   (to the end of the 2001-02 season)

Ian Bishop – the crowd loved him – twice!

IAN Bishop joins, amongst others, such illustrious names as Asa Hartford, Dennis Tueart and Peter Barnes as having two distinct careers at Maine Road.

His first spell started in July 1989 when he was signed by Mel Machin from Bournemouth for a fee reported to be £465,000, a deal that saw City's Paul Moulden move to the south coast a few weeks later for £300,000. Machin had been impressed by Bishop's skills at the end of the previous season when, with the Blues striving for promotion and with just one more game left, they squandered a 3-0 half-time lead only for a Bishop-inspired Bournemouth to fight back and earn a 3-3 draw. Fortunately a draw at Bradford the following week was enough to earn promotion and Machin saw Bishop and fellow newcomer (the one million pounds) Clive Allen as the ideal players required for an assault on the top division.

Both players made their City debuts in the opening day of the season (a 3-1 defeat at Anfield), a disappointing start but one that would improve immeasurably just six games later. The date was 23 September 1989, a date forever etched on the memories of City fans who were then on the day when Alex Ferguson's multi-million pounds Manchester United were humiliated 5-1 in the Moss Side sunshine by the division's new boys. In later years Bishop himself said that it was probably the best game he ever played in. It was a day everything went right for the whole side with Bishop's passing being of it's usual high standard and to cap it all off he scored a brilliant (and unusual for him) diving header to give City a 3-0 lead.

Largely though, Bishop was playing in a side that was at best inconsistent. Despite that terrific win against United the team struggled to find steady form and in December 1989 Machin was replaced by Howard Kendall. If it was a good move for the club it wasn't for Bishop personally. Stories abounded at the time of Kendall taking a serious dislike to the length of Bishop's hair and even if they weren't true it is fair to say that Bishop's style of play did differ greatly than Kendall's apparent 'dogs of war' attitude. Whatever the reasons, under Kendall Bishop made just one appearance before being sold in December 1989 alongside Trevor Morley to West Ham with Mark Ward coming to Maine Road in exchange.

For the next eight years – undoubtedly the best playing ones of his career – Bishop became as popular at West Ham as he had during his short space of time with City. In March 1998 he gave up the offer of a testimonial at West Ham when Joe Royle offered him the chance to return to Maine Road on a two-year contract. It was an opportunity for the 33-year-old Liverpool-born midfielder to try to forget the last time he wore a City shirt. That was back on Boxing Day 1989, City beat Norwich 1-0 and Bishop left the pitch with the crowd singing his name and tears rolling down his face.

Never the fastest player of all time, Bishop introduced the skill and calmness needed on occasion to slow down the 100 mph tempo of lower division games. When he came off the bench at Wembley in the famous Gillingham game, City's whole method of play changed and he was a key player in that remarkable reversal of fortunes. 12 months later he came off the bench at Blackburn to replace Jamie Pollock, City won 4-1 and Joe Royle's side had won back-to-back promotions.

Now 35, Bishop was back in the top flight and had only one ambition left; to return to Upton Park in City's colours. This he managed in November 2000 but unfortunately he was an unused substitute in a game best forgotten as the Blues lost 4-1. The following March he left Maine Road and England and took his silky skills to the sunshine state of Florida to join Miami Fusion in the MSL, a League that appeared ideally suited to Bishop's abilities and style of play.

Who knows it might also give him the opportunity to finally establish his budding career as a writer and illustrator of children's books.

Maine Road career

83-33 appearances   7 goals

Tony Book – the grand old man of football

WHEN Tony Book arrived at Maine Road in July 1966 no one, least of all Book himself, could have known what was in store. Born in Bath in September 1935, Book spent seven years of his young life living in India whilst his father served with the Somerset Light Infantry. It was in India that the barefoot Book took his first footballing steps. On his return to England, Book began to show promise at school and eventually progressed to both Bath and Somerset Boys. After his National Service, he started his bricklaying apprenticeship, all the while still playing amateur football. Peasedown Miners and Frome Town were two early clubs before he played for 11 years with Bath City. It was at Bath that he met Malcolm Allison for the first time.

When Allison moved on to Plymouth Argyle he remembered the softly spoken full-back and took him to Home Park in August 1964 for a fee of £1,500. Book took to League football almost immediately and missed just three games in two seasons before once again joining forces with Allison, this time at Maine Road.

It was 20 July 1966 and despite Allison's pleas, Joe Mercer was reluctant to part with £17,000 in order to acquire the services of a soon to be 31-year-old with no experience of First Division football, the division City would now be playing in following their recent Second Division championship success.

When challenged by Allison about his own age on being transferred from Everton to Arsenal some 20 years earlier, Mercer finally gave in and Allison got his way. It turned out to be one of the best signings the club has ever made.

By the end of his first season at Maine Road Book had won the inaugural Player of the Year Award, the first of many awards he'd collect over the next few years. Speaking at the time, he said he always felt he could hold his own in League football and went on to say that he would be quite happy if he could play for two seasons at the top and then call it a day. Little did he know that when those two years were up he'd be the captain of a side that had been crowned First Division champions and was about to play in Europe for the first time in their history.

An Achilles injury kept him out for the first half of the 1968-69 season but when he returned in January it appeared as though he'd never been away. Within three months of his return he'd been named joint Footballer of the Year with Derby's Dave Mackay and had skippered the Blues to FA Cup success against Leicester at Wembley. Not content with collecting one team trophy per season, he picked up two in 1970; the League Cup and the European Cup-winners' Cup. Along with Joe Mercer and Malcolm Allison, Tony Book had led City to the most successful period in its history. He brought a wealth of experience to the side along with sound organisational skills, a cool head and no shortage of athleticism.

When he finally retired from playing in November 1973, Book became assistant manager to the much-chronicled disciplinarian Ron Saunders. Five months later Saunders lost his job and the former captain took over. The fact that Book had been a player so very recently seemed to ease him into the position without too much difficulty. By the end of his first full season in charge City finished a creditable eighth in Division One and had recruited the not inconsiderable talents of Asa Hartford and Joe Royle to the ranks. Dave Watson arrived in time for the next campaign as Book built a squad capable of again finishing eighth only this time they crowned the season with a League Cup Final win over Newcastle. Despite that win at Wembley, the 1976-77 season was probably the highest point in Book's managerial career. With Brian Kidd now leading the attack (and scoring 21 times) City finished second by a solitary point to a very strong Liverpool side.

Two years later Malcolm Allison returned but the partnership proved unsuccessful. City languished too near the bottom of the table and suffered a bad FA Cup defeat at Fourth Division Halifax Town. Not surprisingly both men were sacked in October 1980. By his own admittance it was Book's lowest point in his Maine Road career. And yet that career wasn't over.

After spending six months at Cardiff, he was invited as a guest to watch the Centenary FA Cup Final between City and Tottenham. The reaction he received from Blues' supporters on that day made him realise just how liked and respected he still was at Maine Road so when new manager John Bond offered him a job on the youth development side, Book leapt at it. It was the first of many backroom jobs he held until Frank Clark finally severed his ties in 1996. Tony Book is now deservedly one of City's honorary presidents.

Maine Road career

306-3 games   5 goals

Tommy Booth – local boy made good

TOMMY Booth was a 15-year-old schoolboy watching from the terraces when City lost to Swindon Town in the now infamous 8,000 game in January 1965. Nine months later he'd signed for the club as an amateur. He was on the books for 16 years, surely a dream beyond the wildest any born and bred Blue could ever have.

In his younger days he represented both Middleton Boys (he was born in Langley) and Manchester Catholic Boys and had impressed chief scout Harry Godwin and Malcolm Allison playing in Sunday League games as a centre-forward. Whilst serving his engineering apprenticeship, Booth trained with City two nights a week, eventually turning professional on 26 August 1967.

By this time he'd reverted to a centre-half role and after steady performances in the reserve side he was given his chance in the first team in a League Cup tie at Huddersfield in September 1968. The following month he played his first League game, a 1-1 draw against Arsenal at Maine Road. He missed just two of the remaining 29 League games that season, effectively removing the regular centre-half George Heslop from the position. City had undoubtedly uncovered a new talent.

By no means a 'stopper' in the old-fashioned sense, Booth used his 6ft 2ins frame admirably in both defence and attack but also showed a deft touch with the ball at his feet. At the end of his first season in the senior side the 19-year-old was playing an FA Cup at Wembley alongside such illustrious names as Francis Lee, Colin Bell and Mike Summerbee. For all the talent and firepower at their disposal in attack it was the defender Booth who'd got them to the Final with the only goal of the game in the dying moments against Everton in the semi-final at Villa Park. The victory against Leicester was the first of Booth's five Finals with City; he'd be on the losing side just once.

Throughout the first half of the 1970s Booth was a key figure in the fortunes of Manchester City and won four caps for England at Under-23 level. After overcoming some back problems during the 1974-75 season he was then confronted with the imposing figure of Dave Watson, a new figure at the club brought in by manager Tony Book from Sunderland who also happened to be England's centre-half. Not surprisingly he missed the first dozen games of the new season but then moved to a midfield role following the injury to Colin Bell. Although a hugely different player from Bell, Booth deputised in his own way. Never the quickest around, he used both his brain and his ability to full effect, and, just like at the back, he never let the side down. When Mike Doyle suffered an injury towards the end of the 1976-77 season, Booth reverted back to the heart of defence and formed a solid partnership with Watson as City missed out on the championship by one point to Liverpool.

At the end of the 1970s and the beginning of the 1980s, under Tony Book, Malcolm Allison and finally John Bond, he averaged almost 30 League games a season, regularly contributing the odd goal along the way. His final game for the Blues took place in a 3-0 defeat at Birmingham on 19 September 1981, a combination of Tommy Caton and manager Bond's son Kevin, finally bringing the curtain down on a Maine Road career spanning three decades. Only six men have ever played more games for City than Booth.

Along with Gary Buckley, he joined Tommy Docherty's Preston North End for a reported £30,000 fee two weeks after his final game for City. He played for three seasons at Deepdale before taking on the coaching role in 1984 and then became manager the next year. Unfortunately his reign coincided with a run of bad results and a shortage of money and in January 1986 he lost his job after just nine months in charge. His replacement was his assistant Brian Kidd, a former teammate at Maine Road. Kidd was less successful than Booth; he lasted only three months.

Away from football after more than 20 years, Booth then set up a sports trophy business with his brother. The venture lasted a further three years before he got a job with Granada as a television, satellite and video engineer, a job he still has today. Still popular with supporters, he also finds time to make welcome appearances at former players functions.

Maine Road career
487-4 appearances   36 goals

Ken Branagan – so close and yet so far

AS a schoolboy footballer there was no doubting Ken Branagan's ability. By the time he'd reached his 16th birthday he'd played for his local team North Salford Youth Club, Manchester County Boys, Lancashire Boys, England Boys and Great Britain Boys. Most of these games had been played against the backdrop of World War Two when Branagan was evacuated well away form his industrial birthplace. With Bury and Birmingham already aware of his prowess, it was only a matter of time before one of the bigger clubs showed an interest in him.

Branagan came from a family of City supporters and it therefore came as quite a shock when it was United who first approached him, signing him on amateur forms as a 15-year-old.

In November 1948, still as an amateur, he was persuaded by Jock Thomson (and his own father) that things would be better at Maine Road and he moved across town – and straight into National Service. Now a part-time professional, City held his registration but gave him a £10 signing on fee 'for life'. His two years in the military took him firstly to Carlisle and then to the ruins of war-torn Germany.

He returned to Maine Road to make his debut as a replacement for the injured captain Eric Westwood in a 5-3 win against Sheffield United on 9 December 1950. By now he was 20 years old and the combined training of both football and the army had made him into a solidly built full-back, one who would give sterling performances for a full decade to City.

His debut season coincided with City's promotion back to Division One (as runners-up to Preston). Branagan played 10 times and would eventually replace Ernie Phillips as the regular right-back for the start of the 1951-52 season. He missed just one League game in the entire next two seasons before being stricken down with appendicitis, an ailment that was to prove costly.

In the year after he got married (1954), City began a run that would take them to the FA Cup Final and a game with Newcastle United. During Branagan's absence Jimmy Meadows began to turn in a string of fine performances that would see him and not Branagan in the starting line-up at Wembley. After less than 20 minutes Meadows was injured and had to be carried off. Not surprisingly, in those days before substitutes, 10-men City lost. Branagan was named as twelfth-man for the game which, in effect, meant he'd play if any of the named starting line-up was either injured or taken ill before the kick-off. He watched the game from the touchline benches still dressed in his collar and tie knowing he was the perfect replacement and yet he was helpless.

The following year was equally disappointing for him. He'd won back his first-team spot only to have it taken away from him again by Bill Leivers in November 1955. Just over five months later City were back again at Wembley, this time triumphing over Birmingham. Once again the pacey and dependable Branagan missed out. To go so close once is bad enough, but twice must have been terrible.

His last season for the Blues was 1959-60, when he played 24 times, the most he'd played in one season since his unbroken run of 1953-54. On 1 October 1960 he moved to nearby Oldham Athletic, the fee reported to have been £10,000 plus City teammate Bert Lister.

At Boundary Park he played the best part of 200 games, his career curtailed in 1966 by a niggling groin injury. At the time he was 36 but still remarkably fit and in later years would say had it not been for the groin injury he could have played for at least another 12 months.

Along with other members of his family he opened a newsagents in Cadishead and began coaching some of the local Sunday teams, including Irlam. It was at Irlam that he received a telephone call from Oldham's Jimmy Frizzell asking him if he'd like to arrange a pre-season friendly between the two sides. That friendly in 1973 was the start of another two years at Boundary Park, this time looking after the youth and reserve teams as well as doing a bit of scouting.

When his footballing career was finally over, he ran a betting shop in Golborne near Haydock for seven years before driving for a building firm. Having spent a little over five years living in Anglesey, the occasional golfer Branagan returned to Manchester at the end of 2001 to continue his retirement.

Maine Road career

208 appearances   3 goals

Jackie Bray – in at the deep end

JACKIE Bray's introduction to Manchester City's first team couldn't have been more dramatic coming as it did in the heat of a derby match, on 8 February 1930. Unfortunately it was to be a losing start for the 20-year-old from Oswaldtwistle with City going down 1-0 at home.

As a youngster Bray had played for St Andrew's School in his hometown, the splendid-sounding Clayton Olympia and the short-lived third Manchester team, Central. It was from Central that he signed for the Blues in October 1929 for a fee of £1,000. Bray was an elegant, speedy and imaginative left-half who played in just two games in his first season, one in which City finished third in the First Division behind champions Sheffield Wednesday, a side that sealed the title with a convincing 5-1 win at Maine Road on the last day of the season. For the record, Bray did not play that day.

The following season, 1930-31 he vied for his place in the side with Scotland's captain Jimmy McMullan as both shared an impressive half-back line with Sam Cowan and another newcomer, one Matt Busby. It was a similar story for the next two years, but by the time Wembley 1933 came around, McMullan had moved to inside-left with Bray establishing himself at left-half. With City losing the Final 3-0 to Everton, the occasion is perhaps better remembered for another reason; a first at Wembley. It was the first time players had worn numbers on their backs in an FA Cup Final. Everton were numbered 1 to 11 and City (goalkeeper Len Langford first) 22 to 12, thereby making Bray number 17.

12 months later (minus numbers this time) City and Bray were back at Wembley, this time with greater success. Captain Cowan had been true to his famous words after the Everton defeat as indeed his side did 'come back and win it' with a 2-1 scoreline over Portsmouth. It was Bray's first winners' medal in the game, but when added to his runners-up one, his six England caps and representing the Football League on five other occasions, he was building up quite an impressive collection.

By the time his next medal came along (a First Division championship one in 1936-37) Bray had missed just nine League games in three seasons and at 27 had become a permanent fixture in a hugely talented City side. In a style some might say typical of City (and despite scoring more goals than any other side in the Division) they suffered relegation the very next term.

Like countless others, Bray's first-class career was halted when Hitler's troops marched into Poland in September 1939. His time spent in the army though failed to prevent him entirely from turning out for the Blues. With 177 wartime League and Cup appearances, only two other played more games for City during the hostilities.

When League football commenced again in the 1946-47 season Bray was 37 and perhaps not surprisingly found himself playing for the reserves. After nine games in the Central League he finally retired from playing and became manager of Third Division South side Watford. Unfortunately his time at Vicarage Road was less successful than his time at Maine Road. After only 11 months with a struggling Watford he returned north and a coaching spell with Nelson that lasted even less (just seven months). He later coached the Great Britain Police XI and showed his prowess as a cricketer as a regular with Accrington in the Lancashire League. In later years (and when his more active days were behind him) Bray kept in touch with sport in general by running his own sports outfitters shop in Nelson.

Jackie Bray passed away at his home in Blackburn on 20 November 1982 aged 73.

Maine Road career

280 appearances   10 goals   (not including wartime games)

Ian Brightwell — "I just wellied it!"

IAN Brightwell was on the books at Maine Road for 16 years from 1982 until 1998 and saw nearly as many managers.

The son of Olympic athletes Ann Packer and Robbie Brightwell had been spotted by the Blues initially at a soccer school in Macclesfield and was invited down to Maine Road for trials. Having passed the trials, 'Bob' soon found himself playing next to other talented teenagers such as David White, Steve Redmond, Paul Lake and Andy Hinchcliffe in City's junior sides. Little did any of them know then that all five would progress through to City's first team.

Born in Lutterworth on 9 April 1968 (just a few weeks before City's championship decider at Newcastle) the two-year-old Brightwell moved north with his family when Brightwell senior was asked to set up the UK headquarters of Adidas in Poynton. With such famous and sports-inclined parents, it was no real surprise when Brightwell turned into a more than competent middle distance runner at school. Fortunately he was also a good footballer and athletics loss was football's (and City's in particular) gain when he signed associate schoolboy forms in September 1982.

With the players mentioned above, Brightwell formed the heart of a very strong City youth side in the mid-1980s, one that proved good enough to win the competition in 1986. On 23 August that year he'd progressed into the first team when manager Jimmy Frizzell gave him his debut opportunity on the opening day of the new season, a 3-1 home win against Wimbledon. He took part in a further 15 League games that season (scoring just once, at Norwich on Valentine's Day), one that ultimately proved disappointing as the Blues were relegated along with Leicester and Aston Villa.

Ultimately relegation cost Frizzell his job. His replacement was Mel Machin, a man who took two seasons to get City back to the top division. By the time 'hostilities' with Manchester United came around again in September 1989 Brightwell had become a first-team regular, capable of playing almost anywhere but by his own admittance preferring either right-back or central defence. The famous 5-1 victory over United will be forever remembered by City fans who witnessed it as well as by Brightwell who took part in it. He once described that game as the highlight of his career at Maine Road although no one could really blame him had he chosen the return game at Old Trafford the following February.

By then Howard Kendall was in charge of City for his first 'derby' and he had to suffer as the home side took the lead through Clayton Blackmore's diving header. Five minutes later the Blues were level thanks to a stunning 25-yard left-footer from Brightwell. With all due respect to the player himself, it was a goal that would have done justice to many more prolific goalscorers. In his usual modest way, Brightwell said after the game, "I just closed my eyes and wellied it!" His celebratory leap immediately afterwards suggested he could have been a good high-jumper as well if he'd put his mind to it!

In January 1993 he suffered a serious knee injury during a 4-0 FA Cup win at Reading. Brightwell would take three operations and 14 months to recover. He next appeared for City at Oldham in March 1994, lining up for the first time alongside his younger brother David in the senior side.

As the years went by and manager's came and went, the name of Ian Brightwell was always either in, or on the edge, of City's first team. This must surely be a compliment in itself as it meant he had the ability and willingness to perform any duties asked of him by a string of different managers; a fact they all recognised.

In June 1998, after City's relegation to the third tier of English football, Brightwell finally found himself surplus to requirements at Maine Road and signed a two-year deal with Premiership side Coventry. His last appearance in a City shirt was in his own testimonial game against Sunderland when more than 7,000 turned up to show their appreciation of his service and loyalty to the club.

After Coventry he moved to Walsall and is currently plying his trade with Stoke City.

Maine Road career

337-45 appearances   19 goals

Eric Brook – all-time leading goalscorer

STANDING at just 5ft 6ins tall, Eric Brook played nearly 500 games for the Blues and is the club's all-time leading goalscorer. The majority of these games saw him play as an outside-left although manager Peter Hodge and later Wilf Wild both encouraged him to 'wander' and almost to shoot at will. He possessed a fierce shot and although primarily a striker, such was his all-round ability that he was more than capable of playing left-back as well as goalkeeper. He found the net 177 times during his 12 seasons (including eight hat-tricks) as a City player and had it not been for the outbreak of war in September 1939 (when Brook was still only 31) it's fair to assume that he would have gone on and reached the magical two hundred figure. It is difficult to say for certain whether or not Brook will ever be overtaken in the Maine Road goalscoring stakes. Anyone who does manage it will have to average almost 15 strikes a season for the same period.

Born in the Yorkshire town of Mexborough, Brook joined City on 16 March 1928 along with his Barnsley teammate Freddie Tilson in a joint deal worth £6,000. At the time it was reported that both players were close to signing for neighbours United but fortunately for City times were hard at Old Trafford and they failed to raise the necessary fee. He made his debut alongside Tilson in a 2-0 home win against Grimsby Town just 24 hours after signing. His first goal came two games later in a 5-3 win against Clapton Orient. By the end of that 1927-28 season Brook had established himself in the first team and won a Second Division championship medal with a City side that had scored 100 League goals for the second consecutive season.

Of all the goals he scored for City, perhaps his most famous one came during the successful FA Cup run of 1934. In front of a sixth-round crowd of 84,569 (a record for any game played at Maine Road, indeed for any game played in England outside of Wembley) Brook scored the only goal of the game against Stoke City. The goal came from his cross-cum-shot from almost on the touchline alongside the Kippax Street stand. The ferocity of his kicking meant he was more than capable of the feat and whilst many said he'd attempted it, just as many christened it 'the fluke from Brook'. The trip to Wembley that season meant it was his second FA Cup Final appearance in succession. The previous year City had lost 3-0 to Everton in a game made famous by the fact it was the first Final in which players' shirts were numbered.

He won 18 caps for England during his time at Maine Road (where, like with City, he became the regular penalty taker), a number only beaten by Colin Bell and Francis Lee. This indicates the sort of company Eric Brook can be mentioned in. In the 1933-34 season he scored in every one of England's four internationals including two against reigning world champions Italy in a 3-2 win at Highbury. He also contrived to miss a penalty in the same game. His most prolific season was 1936-37 when he played in all 46 League and Cup games for the Blues and scored 22 times. This was the season City became champions of England for the first time in their history.

In 1940 Brook was travelling to Newcastle (alongside City teammate Sam Barkas) to play for his country against Scotland when he missed his rail connection at Leeds. Forced to continue his journey by road, Brook had the misfortune to suffer a fractured skull in a car crash. The resulting injury finished his playing career but he did return to football, becoming a coach for a while with his home-town team. Brook later ran a pub in Halifax before returning to Manchester and worked as a crane driver at Metrovicks in Trafford Park.

In March 1965, aged 57, Eric Brook passed away at his home in Wythenshawe. Thirty-seven years later, his amazing goalscoring record for City is still intact.

Maine Road career

493 appearances   177 goals   (figures do not include the expunged 1939-40 season, three games)

Tommy Browell – always a 'boy'

IF Tommy Browell lived with the nickname 'Boy' during his playing career, at least in goalscoring stakes, he was most certainly a 'man'. In more than 100 years, only six men have scored more goals for City than Browell, a remarkable achievement when the loss of four years to World War One is taken into consideration.

He earned his nickname as an 18-year-old when, playing for Hull City he scored a hat-trick against Stockport County. One newspaperman reported, '10 men and a boy beat Stockport'. The name was to stick forever with the Northumberland-born centre-forward.

Even in his younger days Browell had earned a reputation as being a prolific marksman. In December 1911 (the year after his hat-trick against Stockport), First Division Everton – and £1,650 – tempted Hull into parting with his services. He stayed on Merseyside for two seasons before an even bigger move (one many thought too big at the time) to City on 31 October 1913 for a fee of £1,780. By the time he joined City he'd scored 58 goals in 98 games for his two previous clubs.

After scoring on his debut for City (a 2-1 defeat by Sheffield Wednesday at Hyde Road) Browell continued his feats, finding the net 13 more times in 33 League and Cup appearances to finish joint top scorer at the end of his first season. Injuries drastically restricted his appearances to 12 games the next time out in what turned out to be the last season before World War One intervened for four years. That 1914-15 season also saw the arrival at Hyde Road of Horace Barnes, another prolific goalscorer and a player who would eventually join forces with Browell to form a most potent attacking force. Regretably that partnership had to be put on hold until the 1919-20 season (when official League games resumed) but then the goals began to flow. Browell averaged 26 goals a season for the next three and the Hyde Road crowd swelled to bursting point to see him and Barnes in action. His most prolific season was 1920-21 when he scored 31 of City's 72 League goals as City finished runners-up to First Division champions Burnley.

He suffered an ankle injury in a game against Birmingham in September 1923, an injury that seemed to keep troubling him over the next three years and limited his appearances during that time to 49. One of the games he unfortunately missed was Maine Road's first-ever, against Sheffield United in August 1923.

Just when it looked as though it was only a matter of time before he left the club, Browell stormed back to full fitness and form at the beginning of the 1925-26 season. His 28 goals in 37 games was bettered only by the 31 of four years earlier. Despite personally scoring five against Burnley and four against Everton, he was still in a team that would suffer relegation. He carried over his League scoring form into the FA Cup as well that year. As the Blues went all the way to Wembley (only to lose 1-0 to Bolton Wanderers) Browell netted a further seven times in five games, including a hat-trick in the fifth round when Crystal Palace were brushed aside 11-4 and two more in the semi-final against Manchester United. Even in the Final itself he was robbed only by a fingertip save that might have changed the game and possibly ended an otherwise disappointing nine months on a high. In all his time with City and for all his efforts, this FA Cup losers' medal was the only prize he collected.

On 15 September, less than five months after the Cup Final, new manager Peter Hodge transferred the 34-year-old Browell to Blackpool. He continued playing until he was 39 before coaching Lytham and then Morecambe, eventually settling down on the Fylde coast to become a tram driver.

He died on 5 October 1955, just two weeks before his 63rd birthday, although his name still lives on in Moss Side, adorning one of the closes on the footballer's estate close to Maine Road.

Hyde Road-Maine Road career

247 appearances   139 goals   (not including wartime games)

Matt Busby – fruit boiler

SOME people might say that Peter Hodge is the man most responsible for the position of Manchester United in the football world of the 20th and 21st centuries. In 1928, Hodge was manager of Manchester City and it was he who persuaded a young Matt Busby to forget any ideas he may have had to emigrate to the United States and to try his luck in Manchester.

Busby was born in 1909 in the tough mining village of Orbiston, close to Belshill, north-east of Glasgow. When he turned 16, he, like so many other young men in the village, gave up his education, and went down the pit. Basically there was nothing else for him. Apart from football. From a very early age Busby had shown great skill and played for the wonderfully named Orbiston Cannibals (who by all accounts lived up to their name) followed by Alpine Villa where he collected a Scottish Under-18s Cup winners' medal.

His efforts were recognised by Scottish non-League club Denny Hibs, a team that often attracted the top sides' scouts of the day and Busby was touted as a future star of both Rangers and Celtic. City too had seen him play and were interested in signing him although his mother and her new husband saw no future for any of the family and were all set for America. Peter Hodge though would have none of it and so he travelled to Glasgow where he took Busby and his mum for a meal in the Bank Restaurant and offered Busby £5 a week (in the winter) if he'd come to play in Manchester.

In February 1928 Busby wore a sky blue shirt for the first time in a reserve game at Preston. By his own admittance he later admitted that he was homesick and worried about the pace of the game in England. It was also around this time that one particular Mancunian struggled with Busby's strong Scottish accent. When asked by a civil servant as to his occupation, Busby replied, "Footballer", only to see the words 'fruit boiler' written down on the official document.

On 2 November 1929, Busby made his first-team debut as an inside-forward in a City side that beat Middlesbrough 3-1. He played 11 times that season but despite making it into the senior side, Busby was still unhappy in Manchester. At one point he even packed his bags in readiness for a return north only to be talked out of it by Jimmy McMullan, who then offered him lodgings at his house.

When the 1930-31 season began Busby found himself struggling to hold down a regular place in the reserves let alone the first team. Even neighbours United had the audacity to offer £150 for his services during these lean times. An injury to the regular right-half Matt Barrass though changed things. Hodge made the decision to bring Busby back from relative obscurity and play him in what at the time was a strange position for him. Almost immediately Busby's true ability came through and he played in 20 League games that term. Right-half (almost by accident) proved to be his best position. Busby began once again to enjoy his football and any thoughts of returning home vanished. Within a few short weeks fans and fellow players alike were commenting on the way he seemed to control the game and his distribution. Curiously enough for a right-sided player, some said Busby's left foot was his strongest. In 1931-32 he missed just one of the 42 League games and in March scored his first senior goal in a 1-1 draw at West Ham.

The end of the following season saw Busby appearing at Wembley although he had to make do with a losers' medal as Dixie Dean's Everton beat City 3-0. Twelve months later he was collecting a winners' one; City triumphing over Portsmouth 2-1. By March 1936 Busby was a regular feature in City's starting line-up and it came as a huge surprise when the club sold him to Liverpool for £8,000. Contemporary reports suggest that it was the player (stating amongst other things the ill health of his wife at the time) who prompted the move rather than the club.

Busby captained Liverpool for a while but the outbreak of war in 1939 curtailed his professional career although he was to play several times for the British Army team alongside future adversary – but great friend – Joe Mercer. In February 1945 he arrived back in Manchester, this time though as manager of Manchester United. He signed a three-year deal at £750 a year.

A legend in the annals of world soccer, let alone Manchester City, died aged 84 in January 1994.

Maine Road career

227 games   14 goals

Tommy Caton – things might have been so different

GOALKEEPER Joe Corrigan played in all 42 League games of the 1979-80 season. Only one other player equalled that feat; that was Tommy Caton. Nothing too unusual there, many players before and since have gone right through a season but in Caton's case it was a bit different. When he made his debut in a goalless draw with Crystal Palace in August, he was still two months short of his 17th birthday. Not content with his first team duties, Caton also continued to captain City's Youth team, a side that reached the Final of the FA Youth Cup.

Malcolm Allison has been criticised many times for his infamous 'clearout' on his return to Maine Road but little has been said about his willingness to give youth their chance. Caton was one example of this; Nicky Reid had been another five months earlier. Interestingly enough Caton had impressed Allison so much that he wanted him to play in the senior side the previous season but failed to get the necessary permission from the education authorities.

Born in Liverpool on 6 October 1962, Caton's footballing ability coupled with a physique beyond his years made him a target for both Merseyside teams as a schoolboy. Also interested were Manchester United but when Caton and his family saw the atmosphere and general friendliness of City, it was enough to impress the youngster enough to put pen to paper and sign apprentice professional forms in July 1979. On his 16th birthday he'd already done enough to be offered professional terms. The England selectors also noticed his abilities and by the end of his first season he was the owner of four Youth caps to go alongside the 10 he'd already won at schoolboy level. Many felt it was only a matter of time before Caton would become an England regular.

When Allison left in October 1980, his replacement John Bond also recognised Caton's talents and continued to play him. Despite missing the best part of two months with an ankle injury midway through the season, Caton was at the heart of a Blues' defence and was back to full fitness when City reached Wembley for the Centenary FA Cup Final against Tottenham. After a 1-1 draw, City lost to an Argentinean-inspired Spurs in the replay; it was Caton's fourth Final (two with the Youth side) and the fourth time he'd been on the losing side.

After two years of mid-table stability, City were relegated with Swansea and Brighton in May 1983. Not surprisingly the 20-year-old Caton thought his chances of playing for England would be hampered by playing in the Second Division. In November that year, a determined Arsenal offered the Blues £500,000 (gratefully received under the circumstances) and he moved to Highbury.

Unfortunately Caton had gone to a side with a long-standing reputation as being exceptionally strong in the central defender department. After three seasons and nearly 100 games he was still no nearer to reaching his ambition of a full England cap and was sold to Oxford United (a side then in the First Division) for £160,000 in February 1987. In November the following year he was on the move again, this time to Charlton Athletic, a club destined to be his last.

At the start of the new decade Caton developed a niggling foot injury, one that failed to improve despite frequent operations. It was this injury that depressed him greatly, finally forcing him to retire from the game in March 1993. Tragically, the following month, the 30-year-old Caton had died from a suspected heart attack at his home in Oxfordshire. It was a terrible loss of one so young and talented.

Maine Road career

197-1 appearances   8 goals

Mike Channon – it didn't quite work out

MIKE Channon was born in Orcheston on Salisbury Plain on 28 November 1948 and had played 45 times for England by the time he arrived at Maine Road in the summer of 1977.

He'd signed schoolboy forms with Southampton in December 1965, scored more than 150 goals in nearly 400 League games for the south coast side and had won an FA Cup winners' medal with them in 1976. Add these facts to his 21 goals for England (including nine in nine games in 1975-76), and, still only 28, it looked like the £300,000 manager Tony Book parted with for his services would be a good investment for a number of years. Regretably (and without apportioning any blame to one particular party) Channon struggled to reproduce his best form in City's colours and was on his way back to Southampton just over two years after signing what was reported at the time to be a six-year contract.

Under Book, City had missed out on the championship by a single point to Liverpool at the end of the 1976-77 season. Channon's arrival was thought to be the necessary requirement for the few extra goals and few extra points needed to go that one step further.

His debut came in a dour goalless draw at Leicester but the Blues then went on a run of four successive wins, scoring 12 and conceding two into the bargain. He opened his account at Maine Road with a brace in the 4-0 win against Norwich at the beginning of September, playing alongside Brian Kidd, Joe Royle and Dennis Tueart in what was arguably City's most potent forward line since the Mercer-Allison days of some 10 years since. Two weeks after the Norwich game Channon played for England in a 0-0 draw against Switzerland at Wembley. It was to be his one and only cap as a City player, indeed it turned out to be his final international appearance.

He finished with 14 goals in all games at the end of his debut season, by which time City had slipped to fourth place. It was also the season that saw Colin Bell return from his long-term injury on Boxing Day. Who knows what might have happened had a fully-fit Bell been in the team from the start working tirelessly alongside Channon.

At least from a goalscoring perspective the 1978-79 season was a good one for Channon. He missed just a handful of games and ended top scorer with 15 goals in all competitions. However in January, Malcolm Allison returned to the club, chairman Peter Swales suggesting that his flamboyant style and personality would be the perfect foil for the more introverted Book and his coach Bill Taylor. True, by the time Allison returned, City had fallen to 15th in Division One and clearly something had to be done. With hindsight though this proved not to be the right thing.

The first team players seemed to be confused and losing heart, with several being sold quickly and their replacements proving to be much the poorer relations. Channon himself was placed on the transfer list with John Bond's Norwich offering £250,000 less than a month after Allison's return. The player turned down that particular move but Bond's interest had begun a transfer saga for Channon that would run for the rest of the season. It finally came to its conclusion on 8 September 1979 when he returned to his first club Southampton for £250,000. He'd played in two games of the new season, his last goal for the Blues coming in a 3-2 win against Brighton. Three new faces vied to replace Channon at Maine Road; Barry Silkman, Michael Robinson and Stuart Lee. Interesting!

He spent three more years at the Dell before playing a combined total 13 League games in the colours of both Newcastle United and Bristol Rovers, finally signing for Norwich in December 1992. After two and a half years in East Anglia, Channon finished his playing career with Portsmouth in 1985, no more would the famous 'windmill' celebrations be seen on the football grounds of England.

Nowadays he is a more than successful racehorse owner who also writes a regular newspaper column on the sport and still appears occasionally as a soccer pundit on television.

Maine Road career

91-3 appearances   30 goals

Roy Clarke – 100 per cent Manchester City

IF ever there was an epitome of a one-club footballer then surely the accolade must be awarded to Royston James (affectionately and forever known as 'Nobby') Clarke. He signed for City as a 21-year-old from Cardiff in May 1947; an amazing 55 years later he can still be found at every home game joyfully entertaining the corporate guests, generally enjoying himself and gladly talking football with anyone who'll listen to him. Such is his popularity even today, he's never short of an audience.

Born in Newport on 1 June 1925, Clarke worked in the South Wales mines as a Bevin Boy during the early years of World War Two. From his very early days he'd always shown a keen interest and ability in all sports. Clarke was a swimmer, a diver, a rugby player (this particular career was finished when, aged 11, he had his front teeth kicked out) and was such a good baseball player that he even represented Wales at full international level.

For all these other sporting activities though Clarke loved his football most and joined Third Division Cardiff City's juniors in 1942. Finally establishing himself in the first team after the war, he scored 11 times in 39 outings from his outside-left position and began to attract attention from the bigger clubs. With just one game left of the 1946-47 season he joined City for a fee of £12,000. City won 5-1 against ironically Newport County and with it the Second Division championship. The next time he lined up was against Wolves on the opening day of the following season. In doing so Clarke had established an amazing record and one that will probably never be broken; he played three consecutive games in three different divisions.

Once at City he felt at home immediately and his performances only confirmed the fact that he loved the place. Capable of scoring more than is expected from a winger, Clarke was to be a familiar site for more than 11 years in City's colours as he raced past opposition full-backs before supplying crosses to his eagerly awaiting teammates. His slight build meant he was ideally suited for sprinting but it occasionally proved his downfall when it came to shrugging off various niggling injuries.

The 1955 FA Cup semi-final against Sunderland at Villa Park provided arguably the lowest point in Clarke's Maine Road career. In mud-bath conditions he'd scored the only goal of the game with a diving header before being carried off with a knee injury in the dying moments. Clarke realised the seriousness of the injury immediately and knew he'd miss the Final. He also admits to crying in the bath afterwards.

12 months later, still not completely free from the troublesome knee and decked in a new maroon and white striped continental strip, he finally reached Wembley as City prepared for the clash with Birmingham. Marching out behind his Welsh teammate and captain Roy Paul, Clarke, in his own words, 'was petrified'. Three minutes after the start he was involved in a move that typified the entire 'Revie Plan' and City were a goal up. Despite goalkeeper Bert Trautmann breaking his neck, Clarke found himself a Wembley winner. If the game against Sunderland had been the lowest point, then this must certainly have been the highest.

After 40 League games the following season, he played just six games of the 1957-58 campaign before being sold for £1,500 to nearby Stockport County. He then managed non-League side Northwich Victoria before leaving the game for a while and concentrated on establishing his sportswear business on Wilmslow Road. Clarke was enticed back to City in 1960 to run the club's development office, a job he held for six years before being asked to become manager of the new Social Club at the ground. During his 22-year stewardship the club became on the best of its kind in the country and attracted top cabaret artists such as Frankie Vaughan, Ken Dodd and Bob Monkhouse. He then turned his attention to the City's Former Players' Association where, even today, he is still one of its chief organisers.

Only Roy Paul with 24 has been capped more times for Wales than Roy Clarke as a City player. Billy Meredith stands equal with him on 22 so he only keeps the very best company. No one can confirm that this amazing man has ever retired. He probably never will.

Maine Road career

370 appearances   79 goals

Kenny Clements – unsung but always reliable

NOT unlike Tommy Booth, Kenny Clements was a Middleton-born centre-half who progressed through junior football to eventually play in City's first team. It was there though that any similarity ends.

Booth was tall, somewhat lean and gangling and described as a 'footballing centre-half' whereas Clements was a much more physical player, perhaps what would be now be known as an 'old-fashioned stopper'. Never one to shirk a challenge or tackle, he broke his nose three times during his playing days with City such was his commitment. For all that though it should also be said that he was more than capable of holding his own as a genuine First Division footballer, one who could play either in the centre of defence alongside Booth and later Dave Watson as well as at right-back.

Clements was on the groundstaff with City as a 20-year-old in July 1975 when his ability was spotted and a contract offered. Just over a month later and three games into the 1975-76 season he was in the first team, as a right-back and replacement for Geoff Hammond. His debut in a 1-0 defeat at Aston Villa coincided with the debut also of another young local player, Paul Power.

He played more than 30 games in his first season and was an unused substitute at Wembley as City beat Newcastle United in the League Cup Final of 1976. New signing Michael Docherty kept him out of the first seven games of the next season, but, once back in the side, he would not miss one solitary League game for the next two years. Clements had become a solid and reliable performer in a strong City side that played for three successive years in the UEFA Cup under Tony Book's guidance.

In September 1979 Clements found himself one of the many players now governed by the recently installed supremo Malcolm Allison's 'new broom' policy and joined Oldham Athletic for £250,000. He spent nearly six years at Boundary Park (probably the best of his career) before Billy McNeill brought him back to Maine Road in March 1985. Obviously keen to show his new teammates he was still ready for any challenge City held for him he literally threw himself into his second debut against Middlesbrough and got his nose broken for his trouble.

Having won promotion just a few weeks after his return, the main challenge at City was to stay in the First Division. Regretably this proved too much after two seasons although statistics do prove that it was more down to the lack of goals scored rather than goals conceded (therefore reducing Clements' responsibilities slightly) that caused the club's downfall.

In March 1988 he left Maine Road for a second time, again not travelling too far, this time to Bury's home at Gigg Lane, where he stayed for two and a half years. He later played for Shrewsbury Town and finally Limerick City.

The game will always need solid and professional players like Kenny Clements. It's fair to say that the more skilful players such as Marsh, Kinkladze and Benarbia will always earn the plaudits and become the most popular with the fans. And yet, without players like Book, Morrison and Clements, these skilful players would be unable to perform. Another example of this can be found at Old Trafford where for years the solid Dennis Irwin has performed directly behind the more colourful Ryan Giggs.

Since his retirement from the game Clements has become a qualified driving instructor and can be seen regularly tutoring in and around the Oldham area.

Maine Road career

276-6 appearances   2 goals

Tony Coleman – "We can't have him!"

THE normally calm and placid Joe Mercer was mortified when Malcolm Allison told him about a player he'd love to see at Maine Road in the spring of 1967. The player concerned was Tony Coleman, a fiery left-winger with a reputation as being 'unmanageable'.

Coleman's ability was not the problem for Mercer however his temper certainly was. This was a player who'd once punched a referee and then hurled a bed out of a window whilst on a course at Lilleshall. Despite these and other similar stories, Allison was determined Coleman was the player City needed, one that would provide width on the left-hand side and with it more balance to the side. Fortunately Mercer eventually gave in to Allison's wishes, finally agreeing to sign Coleman from Doncaster on 16 March for £12,350.

Born in Liverpool on 3 May 1945, he'd began his career as an apprentice with Stoke City, playing briefly for Preston and Bangor before joining Doncaster in November 1965. He played more than 50 League games for Doncaster, several under the watchful eye of Allison, scoring 11 times, before signing for the Blues.

He made his debut in a goalless draw at Elland Road, played a further eight games that season and began to impress the City fans with his direct and no-nonsense type of play. Full-backs who played against Tony Coleman certainly knew they'd been in a game. The championship season of 1967-68 was his most prolific. He played in 38 of the 42 League games, scored eight times but set up countless others for Messrs. Lee, Bell, Summerbee and Young as opposition sides were swept away by one of the most prolific forward lines the game has ever seen. The flopping blond hair above hands always covered by tightly-gripped shirt cuffs was a familiar sight in City's colours for just two and a half years, but those who saw 'T.C.' play remember him with great affection.

When his hands were visible they were covered in tattoos, a fact that certainly increased his hard-man image, but actually made him very nervous as City reached Wembley and the FA Cup Final in 1969. He was so worried by his appearance prior to meeting Royalty that he pleaded with Allison to try and arrange to have them removed. With the help of a local doctor, Coleman's hands were quite literally clean when he uttered the immortal, 'Give my regards to your mum and dad' to Princess Anne prior to the kick-off against Leicester.

With two medals in two seasons, Coleman was playing in the best team in the country and yet still seemed unable to keep himself in full check as far as his off the field activities went. When someone so well-known for enjoying himself as Malcolm Allison admits to having the 'occasional difficult moment' with him, it makes you wonder just what Coleman did get up to out of office hours! It seems fair to assume it was Coleman's general 'bad boy' image that ultimately led to his departure from Maine Road. Interestingly enough his immediate short-term replacement was Stan Bowles.

On 1 October 1969, just five months after the Wembley success, he was transferred to Sheffield Wednesday, thereby missing out on the chance of collecting a League Cup and European Cup-winners' Cup medal at the end of that season. The move to Yorkshire preceded further stop-offs in Blackpool, Southport, Durban in South Africa and finally Stockport. Following his retirement from the game he emigrated to Australia where he became something of a recluse, although in later years stories came out that he was involved in the road haulage business.

As well as being a real character (thereby automatically endearing him to the supporters) Coleman was a vital part of the City side of the late 1960s and contributed greatly to its success, if albeit for a relatively short time. By his own admittance Malcolm Allison says he failed to get the best out of Coleman; now that would certainly have been something worth seeing!

Maine Road career

102-2 appearances   16 goals

Sam Cookson – always there and ever dependable

SAM Cookson formed a full-back partnership with Eli Fletcher that served City well for six years immediately after World War One.

Right-back Cookson was a local lad who played for Stalybridge Celtic before joining the Hyde Road club from Macclesfield Town in October 1918 although it took him until New Year's Day 1920 to break into the first team. His debut came in a 1-0 win against Bradford City and he was ever present for the remainder of the season.

A former miner, Cookson's time spent down the pit provided him with a powerful frame and although not a tall man, he possessed more than enough strength in his upper body to make life difficult for opposing wingers who were more fleet of foot. He played in every game of the 1920-21 season as crowds averaged more than 31,000 (the highest for the club at the time) in the less than spacious Hyde Road surroundings to watch City finish runners-up in Division One to Lancashire neighbours Burnley. Whilst Sam was defending for City his brother Jimmy was knocking the goals in for Chesterfield and later West Bromwich Albion.

In a side that featured bigger 'stars' such as the free-scoring duo of Tom Johnson and Frank Roberts and the battling captain Charlie Pringle, Cookson was a model of consistency, missing a little over 10 per cent of City's games in seven seasons. Two games he played in during that time are significant in the history of the club.

The first, on 25 August 1923 was the first-ever played at the new Maine Road ground in Moss Side and the second was the 1926 FA Cup Final against Bolton Wanderers, the first time City had appeared at Wembley. Successful against Sheffield United, Cookson was a loser at Wembley, a game that provided him with his only medal for his efforts in City's colours. He suffered more disappointment a week after the Cup Final when City were relegated. Against the amateur side Corinthians in the third round of that 1926 FA Cup run, Cookson scored his one and only City goal.

Another game Cookson played in is also worthy of a mention as it too features in the record books. Without a manager, City travelled to Old Trafford on 23 January 1926 for the 36th Manchester 'derby'. The Blues won 6-1 to record the highest 'derby' victory to date. As for Cookson and his fellow defenders, they appeared not to be under too much pressure until the 88th minute of the game when Rennox scored a consolation goal for the home side.

The 1926-27 season was another ever present one but one destined to end in arguably the most disappointing way of all. On the very last day Portsmouth and City were tied for the second promotion spot behind champions Middlesbrough. Bradford City were thrashed 8-0 but with Portsmouth beating Preston 5-1 they had done (just) enough to go up on goal difference. Their's was 1.775 against City's 1.7705. Another goal would have been enough. What made it worse was the fact they'd already scored 108, a record that would only be equalled by Kevin Keegan's side 75 years later.

In December 1928, after a further 11 League games, he moved to Bradford City before finishing his playing days at Barnsley. It was at Barnsley when, in 1934, the 37-year-old collected a Third Division North championship medal. A somewhat belated award especially after he'd come so close with City, but, nevertheless one that was thoroughly deserved for nearly 18 years as a professional footballer. What also makes his long career even more remarkable is that for long periods of it, Cookson suffered badly from rheumatism.

It came as a surprise to many of his contemporaries when he died at the relatively early age of 59 in 1955. His importance to the club was recognised in 1977 when a nearby street was named after him.

Hyde Road-Maine Road career

306 appearances   1 goal

Joe Corrigan – just rewards for so much hard work

AT 6ft 5ins tall (making him the tallest City player ever) and with only Alan Oakes making more senior appearances for City, Joe Corrigan's name is forever in the record books. Another record he holds is the most number of 'derby' matches for City; in total he played 26 times against Manchester United, the team he supported as a youngster. And yet he should also be remembered for being an outstanding goalkeeper, surely one of the three best in England during the 1970s. Along with Frank Swift and Bert Trautmann, he is also one of the three best goalkeepers ever to have appeared for City.

Unfortunately his two main opponents for the country's number one jersey were Peter Shilton and Ray Clemence. With these two totalling 186 caps between them it restricted Corrigan's England appearances to nine, a figure thought well beyond him when he first started out at Maine Road in September 1966.

Having signed from amateur side Sale he made his debut in the first team against Blackpool in a League Cup tie a little over 12 months later. At the time he was understudy to both Harry Dowd and Ken Mulhearn and when he let the ball go through his legs for Blackpool's goal on the night, his chances of ever becoming number one seemed a long way off. Apart from Malcolm Allison, no one else knew just how much Corrigan wanted that role and just how hard he was prepared to work to get it.

Working closely with Allison, he embarked on a gruelling training regime, one that not only improved him immeasurably as a goalkeeper, but also helped him to control his weight, a situation that caused him problems on occasion. If medals were given out for determination, Corrigan would have won bundles of them.

By the start of the 1969-70 season he'd replaced both Dowd and Mulhearn and apart from a brief spell five years later when it looked as though new £100,000 signing Keith MacRae might oust him from the position, he was City's number one for 14 seasons. When that 1969-70 season ended, Corrigan had taken part in 50 games in nine months and collected winners' medals in both the League and European Cup-winners' Cups.

In five consecutive seasons from August 1975, he missed just one of a possible 210 League games, in itself a quite fantastic statistic. Corrigan was both a good handler of the ball and a good shot stopper and for such a big man could also be acrobatic when the need arose. Not surprisingly he commanded his area with great authority. He picked up another League Cup winners' medal in 1976 and was still in goal the next time City reached Wembley five years later. Despite being Man of the Match twice, Corrigan ended up on the losers' side after Tottenham's success in a replay.

As City headed towards relegation in March 1983 Corrigan knew his days at Maine Road were numbered. As one of the highest earners at the club and therefore one of its most saleable assets, he found himself being sold to Seattle Sounders in the NASL. Six months later he was back in England with Brighton where he played one full season before a move to Norwich and then finally Stoke City. A serious neck injury sustained on the artificial turf of Queen's Park Rangers Loftus Road ground caused his retirement from the game in 1986.

He took more than his fair share of criticism at Maine Road, especially during his early years, and yet it was as a Brighton player returning to City that he was hurt the most. In response to his apparent (but nowhere near the truth) jumping ship before City were relegated, one supporter called him a traitor. After 16 years as a first-teamer one thing no one could question about Joe Corrigan was his loyalty to Manchester City.

A chance meeting with Howard Kendall brought him to back to Maine Road as a goalkeeping coach in 1990. Two years later new manager Peter Reid organised the behind the scenes staff forcing Corrigan to continue his coaching with Leeds, Barnsley, Bradford and finally Celtic before securing a permanent position at Anfield in 1994, a post he still holds today.

Even though it's almost 20 years since he left, Joe Corrigan is still a popular figure with City's staff and supporters alike.

Maine Road career

604-1 appearances

Tony Coton – another one in a long line

AS for international recognition, Tony Coton suffered a similar fate to one of his predecessors in the Maine Road goal, namely Joe Corrigan. Whereas Corrigan had to compete with Peter Shilton and Ray Clemence in the 1970s, Coton found himself up against Chris Woods and the emerging David Seaman some 20 years later. Unlike Corrigan who managed to win nine caps, Coton never made the full national side and had to contend himself with just a solitary cap at B level. Again as with Corrigan, it wasn't just City fans who felt he was as good, if not better, than those who stood in his way. Perhaps the most confusing element of all this though was the fact that Graham Taylor, a man who'd signed him for Watford, was at the time managing England.

The Tamworth-born Coton joined Birmingham City from Mile Oak Rovers as a 17-year-old in October 1978 and would go on to keep goal in nearly 100 League games for the Midlands side before being transferred to Watford six years later. His debut for Birmingham was a memorable one; he saved a penalty inside the very first minute of the game against Sunderland the day after Boxing Day 1980. For the next two years he vied for the top spot with Jeff Wealands and Jim Blythe, finally establishing himself at the start of the 1983-84 season when he missed just one League game although he'd be relegated at the end of it.

After seven games of the following season a £300,000 deal took him to Watford. It was at Vicarage Road where he earned a reputation as a brave and commanding goalkeeper and one who was not afraid to let his defenders know where and when they were going wrong.

Howard Kendall admired these qualities so much that he parted with £1 million in July 1990 to acquire Coton's services for City. Having replaced the popular Andy Dibble in goal at Maine Road, his settling in period was a difficult one with many supporters unable to accept the man who'd played more than 230 League games for Watford. On more than one occasion he seriously considered leaving and had it not been for the persuasive techniques of the backroom staff he would most certainly have done so. But Coton was a fighter and felt the only way to win these fans over was by performing on the pitch. He did this to such effect that by the end of the 1991-92 season (only his second with the Blues) he'd been voted Player of the Year by the City Supporters' Club. That same season – the last before The Premiership came into being – also saw him recognised by his fellow professionals when he was named in the PFA's First Division team.

Coton was always a committed performer during his time with City and the fans began to make comparisons with the excellent goalkeepers of previous years, a long-established tradition at Maine Road. With the aforementioned Corrigan, and the Trautmann and Swift before him, Coton is quite rightly ranked right up there alongside them.

After serious shoulder and leg injuries (not to mention back trouble as well as the arrival of new manager Alan Ball and the German-born 'keeper Eike Immel), Coton found himself surplus to requirements in the summer of 1995 and moved the short distance across town to join United. Signed primarily as an understudy to Peter Schmeichel (a player who came to City in April 2002), he never played a League game for United and in July the following year he signed for his last club, Sunderland. Whilst playing in match at The Dell in October 1996 he suffered a multiple fracture of his right leg, injuries that kept him on crutches for more than a year and caused his retirement from the game.

After a lengthy recuperation period Coton eventually got over his injuries and nowadays is back at Old Trafford as the goalkeeping coach.

Maine Road career

193-1 appearances

Sam Cowan – "We'll be back next year"

ON Cup Final day 1933 captain Sam Cowan led his disappointed City players up to the Royal Box at Wembley to be presented with his loser's medal by King George V. Having been praised by the King for his team's performance on the day Cowan replied, "Thank you Sir, but we'll be back next year and win it." True to his word, the inspirational Cowan and City were back at the famous twin towers 12 months later, and, with no thoughts at all of that defeat by Everton, triumphed over Portsmouth by a 2-1 margin.

Cowan's appearance in the 1934 Final give him a unique place in the annals of Manchester City Football Club. He is the only man ever to appear for the Blues in three FA Cup Finals; his first, back in 1926 ended in a 1-0 defeat to Bolton Wanderers, so the Portsmouth victory really was a case of 'third time lucky' – at least for Cowan.

The Chesterfield-born centre-half signed for City on 12 December 1924 from Doncaster Rovers. He was a comparative late starter to the game with one story reporting his first competitive match was as a 17-year-old, and then only to help out a team that were short on players. It goes on to say that he also played that game with just one boot! Interestingly enough whilst with Doncaster he'd once scored a hat-trick of headers in a game against Halifax Town.

His first appearance in a Blue shirt was in front of a Maine Road crowd of 40,000 against Birmingham City eight days after he'd signed for the club. He played 21 times that season, scoring just once, in a 3-0 win at Nottingham Forest shortly after New Year. The Blues had at last found a suitable replacement for Max Woosnam, the man who'd been the regular centre-half until injury curtailed his career in 1922. Cowan would be the first choice in that position for the next 11 seasons.

Two years after his first Wembley disappointment (a season that also saw City relegated) Cowan had won a Second Division championship medal. By 1931 he'd also played three times for England; twice against Belgium in 1926 and 1931, and once against Austria in 1930. Everton and England's Dixie Dean, the most potent striker of his time, described Cowan as one of the best centre-halves around and arguably the most difficult to play against. Unfortunately for City, Dean had the upper hand at Wembley during Everton's 3-0 win in 1933.

By the time the 1934 Final came around, Cowan's captaincy and man-management skills had really come to the fore with many saying that although it was Tilson's two goals that won the game, it was really the captain's influence and guidance that had actually won the Cup. It appeared nothing, not even a poisoned toe the night before the game, was going to stop Cowan from lifting the most famous trophy in British sport.

The following season, 1934-35, saw Cowan as an ever-present in a City side that finished fourth in Division One. It surprised and angered many when in October 1935 the 34-year-old was sold to Bradford City for a fee of just £2,000. It seemed a harsh way to end a Maine Road career. And yet it didn't.

After Bradford, Cowan turned out for non-League Mossley before accepting the position as trainer to Brighton. He loved his time on the south coast, so much so in fact that he eventually set up a sports physiotherapy practice in Hove. But for all that he still had a soft spot for City and in December 1946, when manager Wilf Wild reduced his responsibilities to purely those of secretary, Cowan jumped at the chance to come back to Maine Road as manager. At the end of his first season he'd guided City to the Second Division title.

Unfortunately for both sides, Cowan's second coming was short-lived. With him keeping his practice in Hove, it made the job of managing a football club in Manchester doubly difficult and some asked just where his loyalties lay. In the end Cowan decided to return south and resigned in June 1947 to concentrate full-time on his medical career. He became physiotherapist to to Sussex County Cricket Club and accompanied the MCC on their tour of Australia in 1962-63.

On 4 October 1964 he was refereeing a benefit football match at Hayward's Heath for Sussex wicketkeeper Jim Parks when he collapsed on the pitch and died a few moments later in the changing rooms. For a man who loved his football so much, it was perhaps the way the 62-year-old would have wanted to go.

Maine Road career

407 games   24 goals

Johnny Crossan – is he really trying?

THE early part of 1965 provided dark days for Manchester City. These were the days of Second Division mid-table mediocrity, apparently disillusioned and seemingly uninterested players and an all-time low crowd against Swindon Town of little more than 8,000. In an attempt to halt this slide even further, manager George Poyser decided skill and leadership was needed and brought in the experienced Irishman Johnny Crossan from Sunderland for £40,000. The signing of Crossan was undoubtedly a success; unfortunately for Poyser though not quickly enough to save his job. He was replaced that summer by Joe Mercer.

Crossan's arrival at Maine was far from simple. Having started out at Derry (his hometown club) he then played for Coleraine before a move to England and Bristol City was aborted due to 'transfer irregularities'. For his part in these alleged 'irregularities', Crossan received a 'life' ban from the FA and was forced across to Europe to continue his football. He found employment firstly with Dutch side Sparta Rotterdam and then later with Standard Liege of Belgium where he played in the European Cup. In October 1962 the ban was lifted and Crossan got his first taste of English football at Roker Park. He scored 39 goals in 82 League games for Sunderland before his move to Maine Road.

When Joe Mercer and Malcolm Allison took over, Crossan was installed as captain and would lead the Blues to the Second Division championship eight months later. Whilst with Sheffield United some years earlier, Mercer had tried to buy Crossan; now he had him, he was determined to use his influence for the City cause.

In the close season he was the unfortunate victim of a car accident, an incident that seemed to affect his play on occasion although not his match fitness.

He continued to captain City during their first season back in the top flight, missing just two League games and contributing a more than useful 16 goals along the way. A compact and skilful midfielder who knew both how to play and how to 'put his foot in', Crossan was hugely popular with the vocal supporters on the Kippax who altered the words of the traditional Irish favourite *Molly Malone* to suit City's captain. During what was to be a too-brief stay at Maine Road, Crossan picked up 10 of his 24 Northern Ireland international caps.

On top of his car accident, he then suffered with his knee and appendix and struggled to completely shake off the affects of both these injuries giving the impression he simply wasn't interested in certain games. Football fans all over the country do not like players who appear not to try. Understandably they make their feelings known to the player concerned; also there's the small matter of a few thousand people on the terraces who'd gladly take their place. It was this apparent 'lack of trying' that caused Crossan to fall out favour with City supporters.

Mercer and Allison had also noticed Crossan's performances were not up to the high standards of previous months. Just four days after the 1967-68 season had started, he was sold to Middlesbrough for £34,500. He played 54 League games for Middlesbrough in two years before retiring and returning to Northern Ireland where he ran both an off licence and sports shop in his hometown. In later years he got involved in junior football coaching as well as doing some scouting work.

Even if he did eventually fall out of favour, Crossan's inspirational skills should not be forgotten as he played a crucial part in putting the Blues back on the road to recovery.

Maine Road career

110 appearances   28 goals

Keith Curle – coolness personified

THERE was a time at the end of the 1980s and the beginning of the 1990s that Wimbledon Football Club loved Manchester City. In the space of four years City seemed to be in the habit of buying their defenders for vast sums of money.

In June 1988 City signed Brian Gayle for £325,000. In August 1992 they signed Terry Phelan for £2.5 million. Sandwiched in between, in August 1991, was central defender Keith Curle, also for £2.5 million, at the time a new club record as well as making him the most expensive defender in Britain.

Although it seemed to be a lot of money, there was no doubting Curle's obvious talent as a footballer. While not one for shirking a tackle when needed, he was a cool, cultured player who let the likes of Steve Redmond and Michel Vonk be the more physical of their defensive partnerships. As a captain, Curle was much more at home organising his troops, collecting and distributing the loose ball and ushering both ball and rampaging attackers into touch with his pace and body strength. Good in the air and a good passer with either foot, Curle was also City's regular penalty taker for a while, never one to shirk his responsibilities, even in front of 46,000 jeering Reds at Old Trafford. With his obvious good looks (especially in his sunglasses he would not have looked out of place in a mail order catalogue) thrown in as well, it's hardly surprising that he was particularly popular with City's female followers.

Before City, Curle had played for 10 years in League football. Having joined Bristol Rovers as an apprentice he moved to Torquay United and then back to Bristol (this time with City) in March 1984. After leaving his home town for the second time, he played for Reading before a £500,000 move to Wimbledon. Ironically he replaced City new boy Brian Gayle at Plough Lane. In 1990-91 he not only earned recognition at B level for England but also turned out for the Football League.

A string of fine performances by Curle during his early days at Maine Road forced the popular Colin Hendry to look elsewhere for first-team games and forced him to return to his previous club Blackburn Rovers in November 1991. Curle missed just five League games in his first two seasons with City, his continuing run of good form eventually giving him the opportunity to represent England at full level. Coming on as a substitute for Andy Sinton in a game against CIS in Moscow in April 1992, he found himself in the unusual position of full-back, a position he was certainly unaccustomed to. He played two more times for England (against Hungary and Denmark) that year, both times again at full-back. Not surprisingly he turned in performances well below his capabilities and consequently his international career suffered. He never again played for his country. Had he been given the chance in his regular position things might have worked out differently.

At the end of the 1995-96 season, Curle left Maine Road after relegation from the Premiership and joined Wolves. He said at the time he was joining a club that was 'bigger' than City, a statement that was not only untrue, but dropped him down significantly in the Blues' popularity stakes. It seemed such a shame to leave with a comment like that. At Wolves though his career stayed much the same. He was still no nearer to any England aspirations, or for that matter winning anything, and in July 2000 he moved on again, this time to Sheffield United, where, at the time of writing he is still playing.

Maine Road career

204 appearances   13 goals

Bill Dale – another who missed out

A SOLID and dependable left-back, Bill Dale was almost a permanent fixture in the City sides of the 1930s, winning both FA Cup and League championship medals along the way. Like many players at Maine Road over the years, his obvious progression to the England team was prevented by one individual, in his case Eddie Hapgood of Arsenal. Many people (and not just those at Maine Road) thought Dale was desperately unlucky not be given at least one chance.

If he was an automatic choice with City, the same could not be said of his previous club, neighbours United. Averaging 10 games a season for six years, Dale finally decided it was time for a change of scenery (and with it first-team football) and signed for City on 23 December 1931. It was a complicated deal that involved Harry Rowley coming with him, whilst City's Bill Ridding (and an undisclosed amount of money) went the other way.

Dale made his debut for City on Boxing Day, a 3-2 defeat at Portsmouth, and was an ever present in the remaining the 20 League games of that 1931-32 season. Standing 5ft 9ins tall and weighing 11st, he had both the physique and the technique to make him ideally suited to the full-back's duties. He was such a proficient tackler that, at least for a defender, he remained generally injury free during his time with City. In five seasons he missed only 24 League games, a fine return especially in the days when the panacea for all ailments was the trainer's magic sponge and a bucket of ice-cold water.

Contemporary reports suggest he was not at his best in the 1933 FA Cup Final defeat by Everton. Both Dale and his opposite full-back Cann were constantly pulled apart by Dixie Dean's side who deservedly won 3-0. The following year though things were different – as captain Sam Cowan had predicted – and Dale was in City's winning side as Portsmouth were beaten 2-1. He also played in the famous quarter-final tie against Stoke at Maine Road, an amazing game watched by more than 84,000 people, a record crowd for any game in England outside of London.

At the end of the 1937-38 season City were relegated to the Second Division and Dale was 33. Obviously it was time for new blood and the Manchester-born defender found himself on the verge of playing football for the first time in his career outside of his home city. In more than 270 games for the Blues, he failed to find the net once. Mind you with players of the calibre of Doherty, Brook, Herd and Tilson in front of him, goalscoring could hardly have been included in his job description.

He joined Ipswich Town on 21 June 1938 where he played for just one season before the outbreak of war. He remained in East Anglia throughout the conflict, guesting on occasion for Ipswich's fierce rivals Norwich.

In his later years he came back home to his beloved Manchester where he died, aged 82, in June 1987.

Maine Road career

271 appearances

Paul Dickov – scorer of 'that' goal

ALTHOUGH City won the First Division championship in 2001-02 with some of the most entertaining and exciting football seen at Maine Road for many years, perhaps the biggest single cheer of the season was reserved by the fans to show their affection for a player who was leaving them.

That man was Paul Dickov, a diminutive (at just 5ft 5ins tall) centre-forward whose 110% effort and commitment to the City cause made him one of the most popular players of recent years. When he made a special farewell appearance on the pitch prior to kick-off against Sheffield Wednesday at the end of February, the best part of 33,000 City fans stood and applauded a man who epitomised everything they themselves stood for. The phrase 'he plays his heart out' could have been written specifically for Paul Dickov.

Born in Glasgow in 1972, Dickov began his professional career as an 18-year-old with Arsenal. A player who won representative honours at Schoolboy, Youth and Under-21 level, he failed to break into a very strong Gunners' side and made just six starts (although he did play in 15 more games coming on as a substitute) in six years. With 55 goals in his last three years for the reserve side at Highbury, Dickov also had loan spells with Luton and Brighton before Alan Ball brought him to Maine Road for £800,000 on 22 August 1996, just four days before Ball handed in his resignation. Some cynical Blues said that apart from handing in that resignation, the only other good thing Ball did during his time at Maine Road was to sign Dickov.

His first appearance in a Blue shirt came as a substitute (for Mikhail Kavelashvili) in a strange 2-1 defeat at Stoke two days after signing. The game was strange because both sets of supporters were chanting for Ball's head! With five goals in his first season, Dickov was fourth in the list behind Uwe Rosler, Georgi Kinkladze and Nicky Summerbee but by then end of the following (1997-98) he was top with nine. His final goal of the season in the 5-2 win at Stoke was scant consolation for City's relegation – for the first time in their history – to the third tier of English football.

Little did he know then that just 12 months later City would win promotion via the play-offs in one of the most remarkable games ever played at Wembley and Dickov would write himself forever into the folklore of Manchester City. Personally it was another good season for him goalscoring wise. Forming a powerful partnership with Shaun Goater, 'Dicky' scored 17 times, including a hat-trick in a 4-0 win against Lincoln City.

With a final League position of third, City had to overcome two very difficult play-off games against sixth-placed Wigan Athletic before the final appearance against Gillingham. That game – on 30 May 1999 – typified the Manchester City of recent seasons. Two goals down with just four minutes to go City looked down and out and destined to spend another 12 months in what manager Joe Royle described as a 'horrible division'. Although Kevin Horlock did manage to pull a goal back the game still seemed too far out of reach. When the referee signalled five extra minutes of added time the Blues were further lifted. It was then that Dickov pounced, smashing the vital equaliser high into the net past Vince Bartram – Dickov's good friend and best man – in the Gillingham goal. The goal took the game to penalties but Dickov's personal drama was not yet finished as he saw his spot-kick hit both posts before agonisingly bouncing clear. Fortunately his teammates faired better as City triumphed in arguably – at least for Gillingham – the worst possible scenario.

If that was a dramatic end to the season, unbelievably City – and Dickov – were at it again the next. Needing to avoid defeat at Blackburn to gain the runners-up spot to champions Charlton Athletic, the Blues decided to do it the hard way again. Going in a goal down at the break, City (helped by some very fortuitous woodwork and a Blackburn own goal) scored four times in the second-half with Dickov leaving the bench to score the final goal. His all-round commitment finally earned a full Scottish cap when he played against San Marino in a 3-0 win in October 2000.

The joys of Premiership football lasted for just the one season although under new manager Kevin Keegan City were to bounce back at the first possible opportunity. With the prolific Goater still in fine form and Darren Huckerby and Paulo Wanchope arriving, Dickov's first-team chances became fewer and he eventually moved to Leicester just two months before City were crowned champions. Unfortunately he joined a team that would pass City going in the opposite direction.

Having savoured some awful times at Maine Road, it was perhaps a shame that he couldn't have stayed that bit longer and earned himself a medal. No City fan would have begrudged him one.

Maine Road career
122-58 appearances   41 goals

Peter Doherty – nothing he couldn't do

CITY fans of a certain 'vintage' are extremely fortunate to be able to compare the talents of Colin Bell to a player thought by many to be the only one who comes anywhere near Bell's standing as City's greatest player of all time. The man in question is Peter Dermont Doherty, a wonderfully talented footballer whose best years were taken from him by World War Two. What is beyond question though is Doherty's standing in the game; he was undoubtedly the most gifted and brilliant player of his generation.

A native of Magherafelt in Northern Ireland, Doherty first came to prominence as a teenager for Station United in Coleraine, later joining the town's side before a move to Glentoran in June 1930. Three years later the 17-year-old travelled across the Irish Sea to join Blackpool, so beginning a football career in England that would last for 40 years, and a love affair with a seaside town that he'd later retire to.

He was a most complete footballer. He possessed two good feet, was very quick and fit, could head the ball and was deadly in front of goal. With Blackpool featuring regularly in the middle of the Second Division, it soon became obvious that they would struggle to hold on to their star player. On 19 February 1936, after 28 goals in 83 League games for Blackpool, he joined City for a then club record fee of £10,000.

In nine appearances that season he scored four times, his first coming in his third appearance, a 6-0 home win against Middlesbrough. Three games later, both City and Doherty went one better. Bolton were humiliated 7-0 and Doherty scored twice. After the initial shock of such a large fee, City supporters soon realised what a player Wilf Wild had brought to the club. The next season, 1936-37, was a fantastic one for both player and club.

Doherty missed just one of the 42 League games, scored 30 times and City (with 107 goals in total), were crowned champions of Division One for the first time in their history. 12 months later, amazingly City scored more than any team in the division (80, of which Doherty's contribution was 12) but were still relegated. With Eric Brook and Ernie Toseland providing ample support in attack, Doherty maintained his average of better than a goal every other game right up until the aborted 1939-40 season. Even then he scored twice in the three games played. It was after war had been declared that things began to go sour with Doherty at City. Like every player in the country, his contract was torn up and he had to look for work elsewhere. Unable to secure an engineering position in Manchester he was offered a job in Greenock, Scotland, where it was hoped he could continue playing at weekends. However though, the club still held his registration and refused permission for him to play for anyone else.

Not surprisingly this prevention of playing angered the normally quite and placid Irishman and in the end, after serving for a while in the RAF, he returned to Manchester and wartime games for City. In spite of any animosity, Doherty hadn't forgotten how to do what he did best. Only James Currier betters his return of 60 goals in 89 appearances with 84 from 113 during the hostilities.

Dissatisfied with the system in general and City in particular, he was allowed to move to Derby County (a team he had generously been allowed to guest for during the war) in December 1945. Playing with another great player of the time, Raich Carter, Doherty was an FA Cup winner with his new team just a few months later.

He stayed for a year at the Baseball Ground before a move to Huddersfield Town, eventually finishing his career as a player-manager with Doncaster Rovers. Doherty then had a series of managerial and scouting positions at Bristol City, Notts. County, Aston Villa, Preston and Sunderland, finally retiring from the game completely after a spell as a scout for Blackpool, the town where it had all began for him in England, in 1973. From October 1951 until February 1962 the enthusiastic Doherty took charge of the Northern Ireland national side, guiding them to the quarter-finals of the 1958 World Cup in Sweden. It was perhaps his proudest moment in a long and glittering career.

Having been the centre of attraction and a famous figure for so long, Doherty became a private figure for most of his retirement spent on the Fylde coast. His son Paul kept the family connection with City going in later years, firstly as the programme editor and in more recent times as producer of the end of season videos. Peter Doherty, one of the finest players of all time, passed away in May 1990 aged 76.

Maine Road career

131 appearances   80 goals   (not including wartime games)

Willie Donachie – admired as a player, respected as a coach

WITH 35 Scottish caps to his name, only current reserve-team coach Asa Hartford (with 36) has won more during a playing career at Maine Road. On top of that, only nine men have ever played more first team games in City's colours. It seems as though both those feats will keep Donachie's name in the Blues' list of achievements for many years to come.

Born in the tough Glasgow district of the Gorbals in October 1951, Donachie was a midfielder with Glasgow Amateurs when spotted by a City scout and invited for trials at Maine Road. In December 1968 he signed as a junior and under the watchful eyes of Mercer and Allison's vastly experienced coaching staff, began his transformation into a highly competent full-back, good enough to represent his country in that position at the World Cup Finals in Argentina 10 years later.

Replacing Tony Book because of an ankle injury, Donachie made his first team debut as a substitute in a 1-1 draw against Nottingham Forest in February 1970. His debut coincided with a particularly lean spell in front of goal for the Blues and that Forest game was nearly decided by Donachie himself when he had a goal-bound effort saved towards the end. An inspection of his goalscoring record at Maine Road suggests that if he had scored on that particular day, it would have been more through good luck than judgment.

When regular left-back Glyn Pardoe suffered a horrendous broken leg at Old Trafford in December that year it gave Donachie and then record signing Arthur Mann the chance to battle it out for the vacant position. Although Mann initially got the nod for the next seven games, once Donachie was finally given his chance in March 1971, he'd be the first choice number-three for the next nine seasons.

He had perhaps the ideal skills and temperament for the full-back's role. Not only was he solid in the tackle, he was also very quick and distributed the ball well from defence, his passing ability no doubt a legacy of his days as a midfielder. A string of highly consistent performances for the Blues earned him his first full Scottish cap (he had already been capped twice at Under-23 level) against Peru at Hampden Park in April 1972. In six seasons from 1972-73 he missed just 11 League games and was an ever present in both 1973-74 and 1976-77. During that period he played in both of City's League Cup Finals, a loser against Wolves in 1974 but a winner against Newcastle two years later. It would be his only medal with City.

The comings and goings of 1979 and 1980 proved no immediate cause for concern for Donachie (by now one of the senior players), although it was a difficult period of transition at Maine Road. By his own choice, he accepted the call of NASL side Portland Timbers in March 1980 and moved west for a fee of £200,000. When he returned to England he joined Norwich, later playing for Burnley, before finishing his playing career after more than 150 games for Oldham Athletic. Always an extremely fit player, Donachie played for Oldham when he was more than 40.

It was at Boundary Park that he got into the coaching side of the game and would eventually become number two to manager Joe Royle. The pair worked wonders with very limited resources before being tempted to try their hands on the bigger stage of one of Royle's former clubs Everton, in 1994. Despite winning the FA Cup in the following year, the Merseysiders dispensed with the couple's services in 1997, leaving the door open to take jobs they'd both been linked to many times in the past; at Maine Road.

After an unstoppable slide into the Second Division, back-to-back promotions followed as Royle and Donachie turned around the fortunes of Manchester City. Unfortunately though the Blues' visit to the Premiership was to last the shortest possible time and ultimately it cost Royle - but not Donachie - his job. Asked to stay on by new manager Kevin Keegan, Donachie did so for the first four months of the 2001-02 season before deciding to try the new pastures of Sheffield Wednesday. He went with no ill feeling or much-publicised fall-out. In fact he went with the blessings of everyone at Manchester City. The word accomplished perfectly describes Willie Donachie.

Maine Road career

431-5 appearances   2 goals

Harry Dowd – reflexes and agility

"WE'RE playing Arsenal today Harry, they're the ones in red." So goes an apocryphal story about Harry Dowd's interest in football. Some said he was more interested in his plumbing, a trade he'd qualified at prior to becoming a professional footballer at the relatively old age of 22. Mind you, a certain Tom Finney was also a plumber and it didn't seem to do him any harm!

Signed from ICI Blackley in January 1958, goalkeeper Dowd became understudy at Maine Road to the celebrated Bert Trautmann. It was an enviable position with the German seemingly invincible and another young local goalkeeper, Salford-born Steve Fleet, apparently having first refusal. After waiting three years, Dowd was finally given his chance in the senior side. It was not the most auspicious of starts. On 9 December 1961 he was in goal at Blackburn and conceded four with only Bobby Kennedy providing any consolation for the Blues. Four weeks later, in only his second appearance, he let in six at Burnley. He would not play again in the first team until October the following year.

By that time Trautmann had all but retired, Dowd had worked hard at his game in the reserves and Les McDowall decided it was time to give the 24-year-old an extended run. Like countless shots saved before and after, Dowd grasped his opportunity with two safe hands. Unfortunately he found himself in a City side that was heading for relegation and despite his valiant efforts the Blues slipped into Division Two and George Poyser slipped into the manager's chair vacated by McDowall. Apart from an occasional appearance by Alan Ogley, Dowd was the regular first-choice goalkeeper for the next four seasons.

Three of those seasons were in the Second Division and Dowd has particular reason to remember at least two games during those dark days at Maine Road.

In a 1-1 draw against Bury in 1964, he broke a finger and was forced to leave the field for treatment. In those days before substitutes were allowed, he returned to the action a few minutes later, with his arm in a sling at centre-forward. When Derek Kevan's shot rebounded off the Bury crossbar, none other than the makeshift striker was on hand (no doubt his good one) to stab home the equaliser. If that was highpoint of an otherwise gloomy period, then he was also involved in possibly the darkest day of all. He had the misfortune to be standing between the posts in the infamous 8,000 game against Swindon in January 1965.

The arrival of Joe Mercer and Malcolm Allison in the summer of 1965 revitalised everyone at the club, not least those homegrown players who'd suffered previously. His reward for all the time spent in the doldrums was a Second Division championship in May 1966. He kept his place for the start of the First Division campaign, only to lose it to Alan Ogley midway through due to an injury. It was similar story the following season, only this time his replacement was Ken Mulhearn. Unable to oust Mulhearn, the underrated Dowd lost out on a First Division championship medal but was determined not to give up.

Dowd's replacement was criticised heavily after City's first round European Cup defeat by Turkish champions Fenerbahce in October 1968. The criticism let Dowd back in and by the end of the season he was on the winning side in an FA Cup Final. That victory over Leicester proved he'd lost none of his sharpness and agility with one brilliant save from Allan Clarke lasting long in the memory.

He had a spell of three games on loan with Stoke before a permanent move took him to Oldham in December 1970. Although perhaps a little on the small side for a goalkeeper, Dowd's reflexes more than made up for any shortcomings, and he remained good enough to play more than 120 League games for Latics before calling it a day in 1974.

When his footballing days were finally over, he became a sales representative for the well-known Oldham brewery, J.W. Lees. Nowadays an active member of the Former Players' Association, 'H' is enjoying his well-earned retirement in Altrincham.

Maine Road career

219 appearances   1 goal

Mike Doyle – a Blue through and through

ONLY Joe Corrigan has ever played more 'derby' matches for City than Mike Doyle, a man whose dislike of the Old Trafford side has been chronicled almost as much as it's been applauded by City fans. In his 24 games against them between 1967 and 1976, Doyle was on the losing side just seven times, a scoreline that no doubt delighted the entire, staunch Blue, Doyle family.

He showed a particularly fierce determination not to lose against United although in 1974 his temper did get the better of him. The goalless draw at Maine Road that year proved a most distasteful and bad-tempered affair with Doyle and Lou Macari both being sent off. Mind you the infamous referee Clive Thomas did take all 22 players off the pitch at one point! Just six weeks later in the return game at Old Trafford, Doyle had forgotten about the incident; his mind now was on Denis Law's celebrated back-heeled goal.

The son of a policeman, Doyle was born in Stockport on 25 November 1946. A pupil of Reddish Vale School, he was spotted by Harry Godwin when playing at left-back in a game for Stockport Boys and was offered a position on the Maine Road groundstaff in 1962. The following year he was playing right-back for the young Blues in the FA Youth Cup semi-final. As time went on he established himself in the reserve team as a strong and tough-tackling wing-half, a position he would play in on his debut for the first team in 1965. His debut came about because of a late injury to Alan Oakes. The only problem was Oakes was diagnosed in Cardiff whilst Doyle was still in Manchester and only a hastily arranged flight got him to South Wales in time for kick-off.

In his early days at Maine Road, Doyle proved himself to be a more than useful deputy at centre-forward, and whilst never being the most prolific of goalscorers (or especially liking the position), he was more than willing to help the cause as and when the need arose. During the glory years at the end of the 1960s he still remembered his attacking days, constantly upsetting defenders at set pieces and taking the occasional penalty. Of the 40 goals he scored during his City career, none was more important than his equaliser in the 1970 League Cup Final against West Bromwich Albion.

Under Mercer and Allison, Doyle was a vital part of the teams that swept all before them. The winner of First and Second Division championship medals, an FA Cup medal in 1969, a European Cup-winners' Cup medal the year after and two League Cups, he was held in such high esteem by the supporters that they twice voted him Player of the Year. With only Joe Corrigan and Alan Oakes having played more times for City than Doyle, and only Tommy Booth matching his five Cup Final appearances, he has a quite unique record for the club. Another record he holds is he was the first substitute (for Bobby Kennedy at Old Trafford in 1967) ever to be used in a Manchester 'derby'.

When Rodney Marsh moved to Tampa in 1975, Doyle took over the captaincy. There was no other choice; Doyle leading out his beloved Blues was the perfect match. Under Doyle City beat Newcastle 2-1 to win the League Cup the following season, the same year he won the first of his five England caps in a victory against Wales at Wrexham.

One of the most tireless and wholehearted players Maine Road has ever seen, for 12 seasons from 1965-66, he averaged almost 45 games a year, a true testament to his commitment to City. For one who never shirked a tackle and was considered a 'hard' player (more by reputation than anything else, at least as far as City fans were concerned), it's also remarkable to think that he never suffered from any long-term injury.

In his latter years, Doyle exchanged his midfield role for that of a joint centre-half position alongside Dave Watson, another player equally solid and committed to the City cause. Has there ever been a more reliable defensive combination?

After more than 550 appearances, the 31-year-old moved to Stoke City in June 1978 in a deal worth £50,000. His four years of consistently high standards for Stoke must surely make this one of the best bits of business ever done in the Potteries. He left the Victoria Ground for Bolton prior to finishing his career at Rochdale in 1983-4. Even during his playing days Doyle was a keen golfer, a hobby he no doubt indulges in even more nowadays in his capacity as a sales manager with Slazenger.

Undoubtedly Mike Doyle had a fantastically successful career with City and thoroughly deserved each and every one of his achievements. He was totally unswerving in his devotion to the Blues. He really did sweat the proverbial 'buckets of blood' for the cause. There was never any doubt as to what colour that blood was.

Maine Road career
565-7 appearances   40 goals

Jackie Dyson – the best jobs in the world

IN those seemingly permanently black and white days of the 1950s, long before computer games, mobile phones and a whole manner of other electronic wizardry, young boys dreamt of growing up to be train drivers or airline pilots. Or footballers. Or cricketers. Jackie Dyson seemed to have the best of everything. In the winter he was a professional footballer for Manchester City; in the summer he was a professional cricketer for Lancashire. There is no documented evidence of him ever being either a train driver or airline pilot, but who knows.

In parks, streets and back yards all over the north-west, thousands of boys dreamed of being him. For them he appeared to be luckiest bloke alive, and, he was getting paid for playing the two best games in the world. With the two best teams in the world. Had he played for 'the other two sides' it is hoped he would have been nowhere near as popular.

Born in Oldham in July 1934, Dyson signed for City (for the princely sum of £25) shortly before his 18th birthday and two years before making his first-class debut for Lancashire. He'd been playing his football firstly as an amateur with Oldham Athletic and later with non-League Nelson where he'd established a reputation as being a skilful player with a keen eye for goal. Yet for all his prowess, teammate Roy Clarke remembers him as being extremely nervous before games with his hands literally turning white. A somewhat strange affliction for such a natural and gifted ball player.

He made his debut at Sheffield United in October 1955, scoring City's goal in a 1-1 draw. A further 16 goals and 32 games in all competitions followed that season, Dyson finishing second in the scoring stakes behind Joe Hayes' 27. It had been such an impressive beginning to his Maine Road career that he was in the starting line-up for the 1956 FA Cup Final against Birmingham. Having scored three times already in the competition, Dyson made it four when he scored City's second in the 3-1 victory.

As an all-round sportsman, 1956 was his best year. After his success at Wembley with City, he then proceeded to write his name in the cricketing record books in a one-sided Lancashire win against Warwickshire at Old Trafford. Dyson and his opening partner Alan Wharton were the only two Lancashire players to bat as the visitors were beaten by 10 wickets. To date this is the only instance of this happening in a first-class match. Also that summer he played against the touring Australians at Old Trafford where he took 4 for 17 and then scored 41.

Regretably though by playing both sports, his services were required by both footballing and cricketing employers as the seasons overlapped. He was also the unfortunate victim of two broken legs (in two consecutive seasons, one of which was the result of a collision with his own defender Bill Leivers and in a pre-season practice match as well) and a broken arm. It was probably a combination of trying to please too many people (he played 150 times for Lancashire between 1954 and 1964) and the injuries that affected his form, and he never quite reached the status of 'great' in either sport. Some said he never quite filled his full potential in either as well.

He was released by Lancashire for 'a serious breach of discipline and an act of insubordination and insolence to the captain' in 1960, returning three years later only to be released once again when his 'performances were no longer of the required standard'. No such disciplinary problems are recorded at Maine Road although he was sold to Stirling Albion in March 1961 for £2,000, a fair return on the club's investment of nine years earlier. Although his career got off to a great start with City, his overall statistics show he played more times in the reserves (77) than he did in the first team. In modern parlance, Jackie Dyson would now be known as a 'squad player'.

He stayed with Stirling for two seasons before moving back to Oldham, finishing his career with Northwich Victoria. Interestingly enough he had disciplinary problems with both Stirling and Northwich so perhaps there was more to his complex character than the average fan on the terraces saw.

On retiring from football he tried his hand at many things including working as a sales representative for a brewery and in City's Commercial Department. One of only nine men to date who've scored for City in an FA Cup Final, Jackie Dyson died in the Royal Oldham Hospital on 16 November 2000, aged 66.

Maine Road career

73 appearances   29 goals

Dave Ewing – "All stop at Dave's"

DAVE Ewing was a centre-half in the old-fashioned style; a real 'stopper'. Working on the assumption that if you wanted to get through City's defences and trouble Bert Trautmann in goal, Ewing's philosophy was, "Well you'll have to go through me then as well!" The only comparable figure of modern times for younger fans to relate to is Andy Morrison.

Ewing's solidly built frame alongside the other formidable presence of Roy Paul made City's defences secure enough to earn successive Wembley appearances in the mid 1950s. Such was Ewing's determination to win against Birmingham in 1956 after the disappointment of the previous year against Newcastle that he took it upon himself to act as 'minder' for the injured Bert Trautmann. Unfortunately, in his haste and enthusiasm, Ewing got too close for comfort and felled the German after his injury! Amazingly Trautmann carried on playing after this incident as well. The legendary goalkeeper said in later years that some of his best saves were made from attempts on goal by the involuntary Ewing.

Born in Perth on 10 May 1929, Ewing joined City from Luncarty Juniors as a 20-year-old in June 1949. After spending more than three and a half years in the reserves, he finally made the breakthrough in a 1-1 'derby' draw at Old Trafford in January 1953. Interestingly enough he'd made his first appearance in the reserves against the same opposition. On his League debut, the *Manchester Guardian* reported, "He is big enough, and he is certainly strong enough, but that he is good enough remains to be proved." Dave Ewing was certainly good enough. After Old Trafford, of the next 270 League games (six and a half seasons), Ewing played in 241. He was unquestionably a key figure in any City side of the 1950s, loved by supporters and teammates alike, and possessed one of the biggest hearts in the game. By all accounts he also possessed the biggest pair of lungs as well; his vocal encouragement to his defence at one end of a ground could be heard by supporters at the other. There were no half measures with Ewing. Roy Clarke once said of him, "Not the most skilful of players but one who could kick a ball to the back of the stand when necessary. If we needed to waste time, he couldn't half waste it!" And yet despite comments like these none of his colleagues liked to be without him. Ewing was the perfect foil for the more skilful players such as Barnes, Revie and Clarke in front of him, but generally any City team not including him would have been a lot worse off.

In July 1962, after more than 13 years on the books at Maine Road, Ewing joined Crewe Alexandra on a free transfer. In more than 300 games for the Blues he managed just one goal, against Portsmouth in September 1957. That 1957-58 season saw City experiment with a new system of play (this was after the successful Revie Plan of a few years before), one that involved Ewing playing joint centre-half alongside Keith Marsden. With Marsden breaking a leg not long after it's inception it was a relatively short-lived plan as far as City were concerned. Nowadays of course a back-four is commonplace literally all over the world.

After two seasons with Crewe, Ewing finished his playing career with non-League Ashton United. Under Joe Mercer and Malcolm Allison he returned to Maine Road as a trainer, his later career taking him to Sheffield Wednesday, Hibernian (as manager), Crystal Palace and then Maine Road for a second time (coaching the reserves to their Central League title in 1977-78) until 1980 when John Bond made the changes almost expected of a new manager.

After a long illness Dave Ewing, a player the fans recognised as one of their own, passed away in July 1999.

Maine Road career

303 appearances   1 goal

Joe Fagan – steadiness and loyalty

JOE Fagan will always be associated with his managerial successes at Liverpool and as a long-standing member of its famous boot-room. Yet prior to that he had a playing career that lasted 15 years, all but three games of which were played in the colours of Manchester City.

Two years before Fagan's arrival at Maine Road in 1938, another player had left Maine Road destined to become a successful manager with another club. The other player was Matt Busby. Obviously Manchester City, and Wilf Wild in particular, were the best people to learn from.

Raised in the Litherland area of Liverpool, Fagan actually signed on 8 October from amateur side Earlstown Bohemians. After a successful beginning with the reserves, he was 19 when given a chance with the seniors at the start of the 1940-41 season, playing the first five games before His Majesty's Navy called on his services for the rest of the war. Unfortunately games played in the wartime North Regional League do not count in the official records and Fagan would be seven years older when his time came around again.

On New Year's Day 1947, he took his place in front of nearly 47,000 people at Maine Road as Fulham were beaten 4-0. Partnering future manager Les McDowall in defence, he'd embarked on an unbroken run in the side lasting 104 consecutive games over the next two and a half seasons. As far as City fans were concerned Fagan was well worth the wait; it appeared finally as though they'd found someone who could offer the much needed stability and consistency at the back. At the end of his debut season the Blues were crowned Second Division champions and as time went on they seemed to have established themselves once again in the First Division with finishing positions of 10th and 7th in the two following campaigns.

The 1949-50 season undid all the good work that had been done earlier. City scored a miserly 36 times in 42 games and not surprisingly were relegated. It cost manager Jock Thomson his job, with Fagan's former teammate Les McDowall taking over. One of McDowall's first signings was the powerful central-defender Roy Paul from Swansea. The relegation and Paul's arrival meant the end of was in sight for Fagan as far as City were concerned.

After playing just five games of the 1950-51 campaign he moved to non-League Nelson as player-manager before returning to League football for three games with Bradford Park Avenue. Following his short stay in Yorkshire he then played for Hyde and Altrincham before taking his first real steps towards the Anfield boot-room when he became Rochdale's trainer. His manager at Spotland was Harry Catterick, a man who would later win the championship with Liverpool's arch rivals Everton. It was actually on Catterick's recommendations that Fagan was offered the position of assistant trainer at Anfield in 1958, 18 months before the arrival of Bill Shankly to begin his revitalisation of a struggling Second Division side. For the next 25 years Fagan and Anfield were one and the same. He held a variety of positions over that period before becoming assistant manager to Bob Paisley following the retirement of Shankly in 1974.

Nine years later, by now aged 62, Fagan was finally given sole charge when Paisley retired to become a director. It was probably his proudest moment, and, like he did more than 150 times for City, he was determined to do his best. His first season in charge was astonishing to say the least. Liverpool won an unprecedented treble and 'Uncle Joe' was named Manager of the Year.

His second season, 1984-85, proved to be his last in football. Defending the European Cup in the Final against Juventus, the tragic events at the Heysel Stadium in Brussels had a deep and lasting effect on Fagan and he retired shortly afterwards. It was such a shame a wonderful career should end in these awful circumstances.

Not surprisingly Joe Fagan will always be connected with Liverpool; and quite rightly so. What should not be forgotten though is where he learned his trade. After an illness, Fagan passed away on 2 July 2001, aged 80. The game had lost another of its best-loved and most respected figures.

Maine Road career

170 appearances   2 goals

Fionan 'Paddy' Fagan – a real livewire

EVEN though Paddy Fagan is now in his 70s he still seems to have an unlimited and enviable supply of energy. Having witnessed first hand him throwing himself around the dance floor at various Former Players' functions in recent times, one can only imagine what must have gone through the minds of many a distressed full-back in the 1950s.

Not doubt given considerable guidance and encouragement by his father (a former Shamrock Rovers and Ireland player himself), Fagan began to develop his nimbleness with both feet when he was growing up in Dublin. Playing for his local team Transport FC, his skilful wing play brought him to the attention of scouts from the mainland, not least Hull City who signed him in March 1951, three months before his 21st birthday.

Two seasons later (after 2 goals in 26 games) he left the lower reaches of the Second Division and East Yorkshire and moved to the lower reaches of the First Division and Manchester, signing for City on Christmas Eve 1953. Les McDowall generously gave him the next day off but then had his latest signing lining up on the right-wing in readiness for the kick-off against Sheffield United on Boxing Day. Although he started his career out on the right he was equally adapt on the left (particularly when Roy Clarke was absent), a facet of his game that was to be of great use to City for almost six seasons.

By the time the 1954-55 season had started, Fagan had established himself in the first team. The season though did not get off to the best of starts with the new Revie Plan coming unstuck with a 5-0 defeat at Preston on the opening day. However, once that little wrinkle had been ironed out (and Ken Barnes had been brought in) the plan gave City its best season for six years with an increase of 10 places on the previous one and a Wembley Cup Final at the end of it. On a personal note too, it was Fagan's best-ever at Maine Road. Not only did he play more games that time than any other (42 in total) and score more goals (11) than in any other, he also scored twice in a superb 5-0 win against Manchester United at Old Trafford in February. These two were in addition to the one he scored in City's 3-2 win at Maine Road in September.

Wembley though has no great personal memories for the tricky Irishman. Although he played in the 1955 game against Newcastle (City coming out on to the famous Wembley turf as the first side ever to wear tracksuits in a Final), he finished on the losing side. 12 months later Roy Clarke had recovered from injury and kept him out of a winning side; such is a footballer's lot.

Despite the emerging young Colin Barlow gradually becoming more and more of a feature on the wing, Fagan continued playing regularly at Maine Road until March 1960 when he joined Derby County for a fee reported to be £8,000. He won two of his eight Ireland caps whilst with City. After 24 games in a little over a year with Derby County the 30-year-old moved into non-League football, firstly with Altrincham, then Northwich Victoria and finally Ashton United.

In recent times Fagan has been a key member of the aforementioned Former Players' Association, his enthusiasm rubbing off on all that come across him. If you get a chance to meet him and have a chat, take it; he's a smashing bloke.

Maine Road career

165 appearances   35 goals

Eli Fletcher – more than his fair share of tragedy

ONE of City's longest serving players, full-back Eli Fletcher played more games for the club during World War One than any other player.

His 133 games between 1915 and 1919 when added to his 327 officially recorded matches give him the highly impressive average of 30 games per season for 15 years.

Born in Tunstall, Staffordshire in December 1887, Fletcher began his early working life as a miner, playing his football at the weekends and purely for pleasure. Not surprisingly the hard, back-breaking toil of life down the pit developed his upper body, proving to be a more than useful asset when coupled with his football skills as a defender. He got his first break at Hanley Swifts before joining the larger, but still non-League, Crewe Alexandra.

Playing for Crewe at First Division Bristol City in the FA Cup of 1910, Fletcher was the outstanding player for the non-Leaguers in their amazing 3-0 victory. So impressed were Bristol by the 23-year-old that they immediately offered Crewe a fee of £300 for his services. Fletcher though declined the offer, preferring to stay in the north and take his chances.

On 18 May 1911 he joined City for a similar fee; it was a fine move for both player and club. His debut came in the fourth game of the 1911-12 season – a 1-0 defeat at Newcastle – and he was in for the rest of the season. He became so reliable that he was in the side (injuries permitting) every season for the next six.

He became so reliable and consistent with his performances that he was made captain by Ernest Mangnall, and was felt unlucky at the time not be chosen for England, having in the end to settle for three games for the Football League.

With 'Boy' Browell and Horace Barnes in front of him and the eccentric Jim Goodchild in goal behind him, it was perhaps easy to underestimate the services of Fletcher. And yet for all the so-called stars and entertainers, football is still a team game and no one epitomised the phrase 'a real team player' more than one of the finest defenders of his generation. In 1918 another former miner, Sam Cookson, arrived at Hyde Road to form a full-back pairing that was the envy of others. Many said City now had the best full-backs in the country such was the ability of both players.

In September 1922, Fletcher suffered a serious knee injury in a game at Birmingham. It was the fifth game of the season and the injury would keep him out for almost 12 months. Early indications suggested to the doctors that he might never play again after his injury but they obviously had no idea just how resolute a player he really was. Although many feared the worst, Fletcher was back in action for the start of the following campaign and one of the most important games in the club's history. There was no way Eli Fletcher would miss the inaugural game at Maine Road on 25 August 1923.

For all his success on the field though, Fletcher's life away from football was a tragic one. In a little over three years, he lost two daughters and his only son. When football is taken into context against such awful tragedies as these, it only confirms just what a remarkable career Fletcher had. He was rewarded for his services to City when, as a testimonial, he was given the gate receipts from a game against Sheffield United in 1922.

Fletcher's last game in City's colours was a remarkable (but for all the wrong reasons) 8-3 defeat at the hands of the same team in October 1925. Interestingly enough seven days earlier, the Blues had lost by the same scoreline at home to Burnley, although Fletcher did not play. The game against Sheffield United was his one and only appearance that term, the aforementioned results typifying City's performances in a season they were relegated.

In June 1926 the 39-year-old joined Watford for a short spell as player-manager before finishing his career with Sandbach Ramblers.

Hyde Road-Maine Road career

327 appearances   2 goals   (not including wartime appearances)

Lawrence Furniss – a man for all seasons

HAD it not been for the devotion and loyalty of Lawrence Furniss, Manchester City Football Club as we know and love it today, may never have even come into existence.

Back in the early 1880s Furniss had been playing up front for Gorton and living in a house on Kirkmanshulme Lane in the Longsight area of Manchester. It was a time of much change in football with many teams, not least Gorton or any of its previous reincarnations, struggling to find a permanent home. In 1884, having played for the last two seasons at an area of land in the Queen's Road-Clemington Park area (affectionately known as 'Donkey Common'), Gorton found themselves once again looking for new premises. Furniss knew of an area of land close to his house (just off Pink Bank Lane) that was both available and suitable and began to make enquiries with the landlord. With Furniss's involvement, a rent of £6 for a year was agreed on and Gorton (at least for 12 months) could once again concentrate on footballing matters.

So too for that matter could Furniss. He went back to playing only to have his career abruptly ended some four years later by a serious knee injury. Because of his involvement in the business side of the game already, Furniss was chosen for the position of secretary-manager, the first recorded instance of someone being in formal charge of the club. His duties in those embryonic footballing days included picking the team to its finances, and everything else in between. Fortunately the powers that be had made a wise choice. Furniss proved to have both the footballing and business acumen required to organise a developing club, in fact so good was he that he was President at the club nearly fifty years later.

In 1887 (having played for the previous two years at the Bull's Head Hotel) Gorton found themselves unable to afford the revised annual rent and so began the search, yet again, for a new home. As with Furniss himself a few years before, another player, this time captain K.McKenzie, found some spare land, and Furniss set about locating its owners. Along with another of the club's administrators, Walter Chew, Furniss found the land was owned by the Manchester, Sheffield and Lincolnshire Railway and eventually negotiated a £10 fee for seven months rent. Although nowhere near suited initially for any standard of football, this new area on Hyde Road would be home for the next 36 years.

Furniss immediately contacted local brewers Chester's for the necessary finances required to build a 1,000 seater stand in return for their beer being sold at the ground. The nearby Hyde Road Hotel, which was used by the club as committee and changing rooms, was already a Chester's house and this new stand was an example of many years of close association between the two parties. Geographically though the new ground caused further problems, as it was no longer in Gorton thereby necessitating a name change. In the summer of 1887 Gorton AFC became Ardwick FC.

Over the next few years Ardwick began to make a profit, joined the Football League, signed many players to strengthen the team and established itself as one of the leading clubs in the country. In April 1894 that same club finally became Manchester City. Overseeing all these historic events was Lawrence Furniss.

So successful and popular had the club become by 1922 it had simply outgrown the confines of Hyde Road and not for the first time a move was inevitable; this time to the newly acquired site on Maine Road in Moss Side. On a former brick works and at a cost of £5,000 for the land, a 90,000 capacity stadium (costing £100,000) was built in just four short months in readiness for the start of the 1923-24 season. Lawrence Furniss was now chairman of Manchester City, a club that owned the most palatial stadium in the country outside of the recently built Wembley. Such had been Furniss's contribution to the club over many years that one supporter wrote to the *Evening Chronicle* suggesting the new ground should be named Furniss Park after him.

Possibly the greatest single (or double) contribution he ever made came purely by chance. He was refereeing a game in 1894 involving Northwich Victoria when he noticed the talents of Pat Finnerhan at inside-right and outside him a skinny Welshman called Billy Meredith. Within six months Furniss had signed them both for Manchester City. When City were crowned as First Division champions for the first time in 1937, Furniss was President. How he must have enjoyed the feeling after so much unpaid strife of some 40 years earlier.

Although he missed out on the honour of having the new stadium named after him, it is hoped that the name Lawrence Furniss will be commemorated some way when the club moves to the City of Manchester Stadium in 2003. After all, it's only two miles from where Furniss helped to start it all over 100 years ago.

Stan Gibson – could grow grass on concrete

THE nearest Stan Gibson got to kicking a ball in City's senior side was a handful of trial games for the 'A' team. And yet he was still a legend at Maine Road; just ask any of the players who had the privilege to play on his beautifully manicured Maine Road playing surface for the best part of 40 years.

Both at school and in the navy Gibson loved most sports but, like millions of others before and since, decided to try his luck at football, a game in his own words, he "wasn't too bad at". Although by no means the tallest centre-forward on record (certainly, not even in his wildest dreams could Stan ever have been mistaken for Niall Quinn) he was powerfully built and it was as a number-nine that he had those trials for City.

Regrettably he was unsuccessful as a player with City but more than made up for it in other ways. He turned his attention to landscaping and groundmanship and was groundsman at Chorlton Cricket Club in August 1960 when he got a call from Maine Road offering him the vacant position at the ground where he was a regular supporter. Not surprisingly the true-Blue Gibson was more than keen to say "yes".

Two years later, the 'big freeze' of the winter of 1962-63 (City playing just three games between 15 December and 2 March) followed by relegation at the end brought about Gibson's first real challenge and disappointment as an employee of Manchester City Football Club. There would be many more of both before his retirement.

In later years of course he supervised a highly efficient under-soil heating system that involved digging up his hallowed turf but ensured postponements by snow and ice were completely eliminated. He would also cringe when the players had the audacity to run over it! Just about able to stomach this intrusion on match days, he was less than keen when they trained on it during the week as he was making his preparations. During the many phases of construction that took place whilst Gibson was at Maine Road, he was always there, pitchfork at the ready, waiting, should some errant bulldozer decide to take a short cut over his grass. However his worst dislike of all was the dreaded summer pop concert. Understanding and appreciating the financial implications for the club, he loathed even the thought of all those people trampling across the specially laid down boards not to mention the sheer weight of the stage and all its equipment. On more than one occasion the Platt Lane end of the pitch was considerably lower after the event than before it, a situation that caused Gibson more than a few headaches and late nights.

But, come the start of the season, everyone knew that the pitch as usual would be immaculate. Even at the end of the season, every season, it was in wonderful condition. Club secretary Bernard Halford once said of him, "He could grow grass on concrete." If he'd have put his mind to it he probably could have. During the halcyon days of Joe Mercer and Malcolm Allison, Mike Summerbee described Gibson as, "another one of the team", such were his efforts appreciated by the players.

After all the hours put in on the pitch (and at the training facilities at Platt Lane) Gibson would go home to his little house sandwiched between the souvenir shop and ticket office at Maine Road. It was here that he sadly passed away on Christmas Eve 2001 aged 76, having retired just a couple of years earlier. He was a smashing bloke, one everybody knew and liked and one no one had a bad word for. The news devastated not only his family (his daughter Janice is almost an institution in the club shop) and everyone at Maine Road, but also thousands of City supporters, for whom Stan Gibson always found a couple of minutes to talk football to.

Billy Gillespie – a bit of a boy

BY all accounts Billy Gillespie was a 'character' both on and off the football field. Born in Strathclyde sometime in the late 1870s, he was the most fearsome of centre-forwards, a man who felt no compassion when bundling both ball and player either over the touchline or into the net. Nowadays of course his style of play would probably mean he'd never finish a game (maybe not even a half) but in the more physical and lenient days long since past, his City teammates, and particularly their supporters, loved him for his aggressive style of play. The same could not be said of the opposition though. Many said he was a dirty player, although had he ever been available for transfer, these same clubs would have rushed forward in droves with the required finances.

No historians are quite sure how he arrived at Lincoln as a 20-year-old, but what is documented is his transfer to Hyde Road. This took place on 7 January 1897, two days before his debut, a 3-1 defeat at Darwen. For all his hustle and bustle and physical approach to the game – woe betide anyone who got in his way – Gillespie was also a prolific goalscorer. The goal he scored on his debut was the first of more than 130 he'd score for City, a figure bettered only by seven others.

Serviced from both wings by the talents of Meredith and Booth, Gillespie's popularity grew so much at Hyde Road that it was second only to that of the great Welshman. He seemed to epitomise the working class hero and as such he endeared himself to the masses crammed into the Popular Side. Also, like the majority of working class men, he enjoyed a drink. In fact he enjoyed it so much that he was dropped at times for being under the influence. Some contemporary reports indicate that wasn't always true; they claimed he was drunk during some games as well! Another problem he faced off the pitch was his control (or rather lack of control) of money. Fortunately Meredith became arguably his best friend in Ardwick and managed not only to sort out a bank account for Gillespie but also took him away on isolated fishing trips on more than one occasion.

And yet for all his off the field 'shenanigans' he was an amazingly consistent performer when it came to match days. He finished top scorer in four of his nine seasons with City, collecting two Second Division championship and an FA Cup winners' medal along the way. In April 1902 he scored all four in a 4-1 win at Blackburn, undoubtedly the highlight of the season both personally and for the club; City were relegated seven days later. His most prolific scoring season was 1902-03 (the very next one) when he scored 30 goals in 33 League and Cup appearances, the season City won the Second Division title.

He was one of 17 players fined and suspended in the aftermath of the alleged bribery scandal of 1905. So disgusted was Gillespie with the way City had been treated, he refused to pay the £50 fine and never played football again. If his career before City is somewhat sketchy, the same could be said for his life afterwards. What is known is that he emigrated to South Africa in the summer of 1905, along with his new bride, allegedly to make his fortune in the diamond mines. Years later he turned up as an electrician in Canada. His swift departure from these shores even shocked his brother Matt, at the time a player with Ardwick's arch rivals Newton Heath. Apart from a return to England for a short holiday in 1934, very little else is known about Gillespie's life, or for that matter his death. However his life fared, if his known life is anything to go by, it would most certainly have been both colourful and unorthodox. If any reader can throw some light on this undoubtedly controversial character, please contact me care of the publishers. Like a lot of other City fans, I'd love to know more about him.

Hyde Road career

231 appearances   132 goals

Shaun Goater – keep feeding him

LEONARD Shaun Goater's arrival at Maine Road back in March 1998 was greeted initially with mixed reaction by City supporters eager for someone who could score the necessary goals required to stop the Blues from slipping into the Second Division. With more than 100 League goals already behind him, Goater certainly had the track record to suggest he might be the man for the job and although he did manage three strikes in seven games City still suffered relegation. What concerned the fans though was Goater's apparent ability to miss more chances than he converted and his first touch left a lot to be desired on occasion.

Four years later Goater has become a massive cult figure amongst supporters and choruses of "Feed the Goat and he will score" have been heard on terraces the length and breadth of the land. Quite simply, Goater is a natural goalscorer; a player who has worked tirelessly to improve all aspects of his game and has been rewarded accordingly. And yet he is not only an out an out attacker, he is also a marvellous team player, constantly creating spaces for his attacking partners as well as being a more than capable defender, especially from set pieces.

Born in Hamilton, Bermuda on 25 February 1970, Goater's first taste of English football came as a youth player with Manchester United. Released by the Old Trafford club in 1989 he joined Rotherham where people first learned of his goalscoring prowess. With seventy goals in just over 200 League appearances in six years, Goater became one of the most prolific strikers in the lower divisions and was eventually transferred to Joe Jordan's Bristol City in July 1996. At Ashton Gate he averaged a goal every other game in his two seasons before Joe Royle brought him to Maine Road for what has proved to be a bargain £400,000. By the end of the 2001-02 season, Goater had scored 97 times for the Blues in a little over 180 games, truly a phenomenal ratio and one bettered only by an elite number of strikers.

In each of his four full seasons to date he has finished top scorer and this includes his one and only Premiership skirmish (2000-01) when injuries restricted him to just half the campaign. Last season (2001-02) proved his most prolific to date when his 32 goals made him the first player to reach the magical 30 mark since Francis Lee back in back in 1971-72. And Goater is by no means the first-choice penalty taker!

For a while in the spring of 2002 it looked as though that elusive 30th goal would never come. With just one League goal in his previous eight outings, Goater was experiencing a veritable drought – at least in his terms. When it finally came (on a Tuesday night at Crewe) it seemed as though City's entire following had willed the ball in for him such was his popularity with the fans. It was those same fans who'd voted him Player of the Year for 1999-2000.

During his time with City he has either scored or been involved in some of the most crucial goals in the club's history. It was his albeit untidy winner against Wigan Athletic in the play offs semi-final of 1999 that set up the remarkable final against Gillingham, a game that looked long lost until it was his persistence that enabled Kevin Horlock to supply the Blues with a vital lifeline. 12 months later in the sunshine at Ewood Park it was Goater's equaliser that inspired the Blues to a 4-1 win and promotion to the Premiership.

The Bermudan international's career with City seems harshly treated if just looked at in purely statistical terms, mightily impressive as they might be. A record that would more than hold its own in any era is only one reason why he is so loved by thousands of City fans. Even his own nation recognise his achievements in English football as well as his work with the island's youngsters and have made every 21 June a national Shaun Goater Day.

A man who scores goals regardless of attacking partner and indeed regardless of division, seems certain in the very near future – transfers allowing – to join a extremely exclusive group of players who have scored more than 100 times for City.

Not surprisingly as the Blues look forward to Premiership football again, manager Kevin Keegan will continue his search to strengthen his squad in all positions. City have (quite rightly) already turned down a derisory offer from Wolves for Goater although at the time of writing the club does seem relatively well off for strikers and has just secured a deal for another with the Frenchman Nicholas Anelka.

Should someone eventually replace 'The Goat' he will certainly have to have that something 'extra' and will have a hard task to match both Goater's goalscoring feats and popularity with the fans.

Maine Road career

173-10 appearances   97 goals   (to the end of the 2001-02 season)

Jim Goodchild – what mysteries lay underneath?

WORKING on the docks at Southampton, goalkeeper Jim Goodchild was very nearly lost to professional football forever.

He'd been born in the same city on 4 April 1892 and had developed his goalkeeping skills playing for his local club St Paul's Athletic. At the time Southampton were still a non-League side although they'd achieved remarkable success even with their limited resources by reaching two FA Cup Finals in the space of three seasons at the beginning of the century. Goodchild was felt to be of a good enough standard to be offered a position with the Saints, a decision that was (in the end unwisely) rescinded after just five first team games. It was then that Goodchild found work on the docks apparently destined to be purely a keen weekend footballer.

City's manager at the time was Harry Newbould. Their regular goalkeeper was Walter Smith, a most reliable performer, but one who was currently suffering from fluid on the knee. Newbould, aware of Smith's problems, was informed about Goodchild's situation and decided to take a chance, signing him for the Hyde Road club on 2 December 1911.

The following month Goodchild was taking his place in the stand to watch his new side's FA Cup third-round tie at Preston when Smith's knee flared up literally minutes before kick-off meaning he could take no part in the game. Goodchild was summoned to the changing rooms and, whilst his teammates were already on the pitch, told to get changed ready for action. It was a rather unorthodox way to be told you were making your debut but in the end, it certainly seemed to nullify any worries he might have had. Goodchild turned in a magnificent performance – he even saved a penalty – and thanks to George Wynn's goal in the dying minutes, he came away on the winning side. For the rest of the season Goodchild and Smith vied for the goalkeeping jersey. Fans and management seemed equally as confused as to who the first choice should be as both men were of a similar high standard.

When the first wartime season started in September 1915, Goodchild had finally established himself. He played 130 times for City during the war (a figure beaten only beaten by Eli Fletcher) and became hugely popular with the fans. Thanks to a cartoon of him in one local newspaper he was given the nickname 'Naughty Boy', a name that suited him ideally and only seemed to increase his popularity. Like the vast majority of men in those days, Goodchild was a proud wearer of a traditional flat cap. Every game he'd wear one and it became almost as big a trademark as Meredith's toothpick had been a few years earlier. In one particular game when trying to clear a corner the cap was knocked from his head by an opposing forward. Goodchild forgot completely about the ball and began frantically scrambling about on his hand and knees searching for his missing cap. The reason, simple, no one knew about the completely bald head it always hid. The fans knew now and ribbed him light-heartedly about it for weeks afterwards.

He was an ever-present in the 1920-21 season, one in which the Blues finished runners-up in Division one to Burnley. The last two games of that season were home and away to Newcastle United with the penultimate one at home on 2 May. This was a game when fans were encouraged to attend more than usual as it was to be Goodchild's Benefit. As six strapping young Mancunians carried a huge sheet around the perimeters of Hyde Road, supporters hurled coins into it, enough to swell Goodchild's bank balance to the tune of £750.

He stayed a further six seasons with City before a move to Guildford City in August 1927. Apart from that 1920-21 season his career with City was spent during a time when no one could question the club's popularity, but had serious doubts about its abilities to be a side pressing for major honours. The nearest Goodchild came to a medal was as a beaten Finalist in the 1926 FA Cup Final. That solitary runners' up medal seems scant consolation for a man who gave so much to Manchester City.

Hyde Road-Maine Road career

217 appearances   (not including wartime appearances)

Johnny Hart – a most unlucky footballer

HAD it not been for a series of long-term injuries, there is every chance Johnny Hart would have been right up there with the best of them in both the appearance and goalscoring charts.

He was 13 years a player with City however these injuries curtailed his appearances to less than 200, or, put another way, approximately 15 per season. During his time though he proved himself to be a more than useful goalscorer, a ratio of almost a goal every other game confirming this point. Statistics go at least some way to suggest he was an unlucky player.

Having played his early football for the amateur side Loughton Youth Club, he signed for the Blues in the summer of 1945 as a 16-year-old. His first appearance for the senior side came in a 5-1 defeat by Sheffield Wednesday at Maine Road in September 1945, the last of the wartime seasons. He had to wait until April 1948 for his full debut in League football, another Maine Road defeat, this time by Bolton Wanderers.

For the next two years he was on the fringe of the first team, playing the occasional game but never really establishing himself in the side. The longest run he had during that period was 12 successive League games from Christmas Day 1948 to the end of March the following year.

By the start of the 1950-51 season new manager Les McDowall had taken over from Jock Thomson and decided to give Hart and extended run. It turned out to be a wise choice all round; Hart scored 14 times in 27 games and City won promotion. For the next four seasons he was a major player in the fortunes of Manchester City. This was the period when his goalscoring ability really came to the fore. Playing alongside the likes of Don Revie, Roy Paul and Bert Trautmann, the Golborne-born inside-forward seemed inspired and for three of those four seasons he was top scorer. For good measure, in the one he didn't top (1953-54), he missed out to Revie by one goal and that came in the FA Cup. His personal best came in that same competition; four in a 7-0 mauling of Swindon Town in January 1953.

As the Blues marched their way to Wembley in 1955, tragedy was to strike the luckless Hart. With 35 games played so far it was proving to be his best season but he suffered a broken leg in a League game at Huddersfield the week before the semi-final. Allowed to travel to the Final along with the also injured Roy Clarke, a further indignity was to befell the unfortunate duo when an over zealous stadium official refused them entry. The damage to his leg required six operations however he recovered sufficiently to play the last game of the 1955-56 season, when City beat Portsmouth 4-2, and, just to prove he could still do his job, he managed to score as well. Unfortunately though the success against Birmingham in the 1956 FA Cup Final had just passed him by.

Everything looked rosy as City travelled to Tottenham on 29 August for the fourth game of the 1956-57 season. Hart had played in the opening three games but then collided with Ted Ditchburn in the Spurs goal only to suffer injuries far worse than the broken leg. He had four ribs broken and a lung punctured. By his own admission, Hart was in so much pain he thought he was dying.

Perhaps not too surprisingly he never fully recovered and only started a further six League games before announcing his retirement in May 1963. However his career at Maine Road was far from over. For the next 10 years – many during the great days of Joe Mercer and Malcolm Allison – Hart was City's first team coach. In 1973 he was promoted to manager, a position he had to resign from after just six months due to ill health although during that relatively short time he did manage to persuade Denis Law to come back to Maine Road after being discarded on a free transfer by United.

With three footballing sons (one of whom, Paul, is currently managing Nottingham Forest), Johnny Hart is undoubtedly a footballing man. However he must surely one of the games most unluckiest players.

Maine Road career

178 appearances   73 goals   (not including wartime appearances)

Asa Hartford – ever ready, tenacious and 'abnormal'

DON Revie's Leeds United team was one of the strongest in the country as football in England entered the glam-rock 1970s. Champions immediately after City, they then finished runners-up three years in succession, won and lost an FA Cup Final and twice won the European Fairs Cup.

In 1972, after five years with West Bromwich Albion, the 21-year-old Scottish Under-21 international Asa Hartford looked all set for a £170,000 move to Elland Road until a medical showed an 'abnormality'. According to the Yorkshire doctors, Hartford had a hole in the heart and the deal collapsed, something that could never have been said about the player himself. A naturally devastated Hartford returned to the Midlands until 13 August 1974 when £210,000 brought him to Maine Road for the first time.

City's chief scout then was Ken Barnes, the former player from the successful 1956 FA Cup-winning side. With only a limited medical knowledge culled from his playing days and having seen Hartford in action, Barnes refused to believe what the doctors of two years earlier had said. He simply commented, "If he's got a hole in the heart, then there's something wrong with all of us." Fortunately manager Tony Book was of the same opinion. Leeds had made a bad move, one that would greatly benefit City to the tune of more than 300 games in a broken career totalling eight seasons.

Hartford's debut came on the opening day of the 1974-75 season, a 4-0 home win against West Ham United. A series of niggling injuries restricted his appearances to 31 in all competitions but it was more than enough to convince the supporters just what a good player he was and what an asset he would be to the club.

He'd joined one of City's strongest ever sides, a combination of players from the glory days of Mercer and Allison and newcomers such as Joe Royle, Dennis Tueart and Dave Watson. In 1976 he played for the Blues in the League Cup Final triumph over Newcastle. Six years beforehand he'd played in a losing West Bromwich side against City in the same competition. That 1975-76 season also saw his most memorable performance in a City shirt. On the way to Wembley, Hartford was outstanding in the 4-0 demolition of Manchester United in the fourth round, a night marred by Colin Bell's terrible injury. With 12 goals as well that year (his best ever return), 1975-76 was a most enjoyable year for someone with an apparent 'abnormality'.

The Clydebank-born midfielder was a real terrier in midfield. A fierce tackler he was also an extremely creative player, one who was more than capable of splitting defences wide open with slide-rule passes. An ever-present in the League in 1978-79, Hartford's gutsy performances endeared him to the fans who voted him Player of the Year as a recognition of his efforts. Somewhat surprisingly Malcolm Allison decided to dispense with Hartford's services in June 1979 and sold him to Nottingham Forest for £400,000. Just three games later he returned north and joined Everton.

After two years on Merseyside he was back at Maine Road at the request of the new man in charge, John Bond. Although by now 31 years of age, he still displayed the tenacity he showed the first time around. He made his second debut in the League Cup against Stoke in October 1981; a tie the Blues would eventually win 9-8 on penalties. Never the most clinical of finishers, Hartford missed his spot-kick on the night.

Two more excellent seasons in City's colours followed before a serious ankle injury meant he could only play seven times in 1983-84. In order to try and regain fitness, Hartford moved to Florida and Fort Lauderdale Sun, playing some 30 games alongside his old Maine Road teammate Dave Watson. On his return to England he joined Norwich and helped them to success in the League Cup.

After Norwich he played for Bolton Wanderers and then became player-manager with Stockport County. Then there was Shrewsbury Town and finally Boston United of the Vauxhall Conference. He played his last competitive game for Boston as a 40-year-old. Whilst watching a game at Burnden Park, a chance meeting in the stands led to a coaching job at Blackburn for two years and later a similar position with Stoke.

In July 1995 Asa Hartford came back to Maine Road. The fact that he is still there seven years later, and has survived the procession of managerial changes during that time, pays a huge testament to his coaching abilities. With 36 caps to his name, making him City's most capped Scottish player of all time, it seems that it was just Leeds United who had the wrong opinion of Asa Hartford.

Maine Road career
322-1 appearances   37 goals

Joe Hayes – "Can I have my bus fare home please?"

IN 12 seasons at Maine Road, Kearlsey-born Joe Hayes scored 152 goals, one goal less than Colin Bell. Only Bell, Eric Brook and Tom Johnson have scored more in the club's entire history.

Despite his apparent lack of height (he stood 5ft 8ins) and at times was troubled with poor eyesight, the young Hayes could never be described as work shy as his early employment in a colliery and at a cotton mill confirm. Despite being turned down by both Bury and Bolton Wanderers he never questioned his own ability with a football and after impressing City scouts in local amateur football, Hayes was asked to attend a trial at Maine Road in the 1953 close season. He suitably turned up at the ground – with his boots wrapped in a brown paper parcel – scored four times and then had the audacity to ask the club for his bus fare home!

It is not known whether Les McDowall authorised this expenditure but Hayes' ability impressed the manager enough to offer him a contract and just eight weeks after that trial game, the 17-year-old was in City's first team line-up in a First Division game at White Hart Lane. The Blues lost 3-0 that October day but by all accounts the young Hayes equipped himself well enough and played in eight of the following nine League games.

He had to wait until midway through the 1954-55 season before finally establishing himself in the first team. He switched from his initial position of right-winger to inside-right, a position that was ideally suited not only to himself but also to the style of play introduced to the side by the ever-thinking Don Revie. He played in every round of the FA Cup that season – including the disappointing defeat in the Final itself by Newcastle United – and had the pleasure of scoring against Manchester United in the fourth round. It was the first time Hayes had played against the 'old enemy' and it was the first of 10 goals he scored against them over the years, a figure matched only by Francis Lee.

The following year – 1956 – Hayes and City were back at Wembley with the Revie Plan now in full swing and it was Hayes' himself who scored the Blues' first goal in the 3-1 triumph. He scored 27 times in all competitions that season making him easily the top scorer, 10 in front of second-placed Jackie Dyson. His continuing goalscoring efforts earned him two England Under-23 caps in 1958 (against Wales and Scotland) as well as a call-up for the Football League.

Hayes also has the honour of being City's first-ever scorer in the Football League Cup. In its inaugural season, 1960-61, Hayes and Denis Law with two were on the scoresheet in the 3-0 win against Stockport County. With an assortment of transfers and injuries, the successful City team of the mid-1950s began to break up as the new decade arrived. Throughout the dark days of the early 1960s Hayes remained loyal to the club only to see his own personal career effectively curtailed by injury. In a collision with Bury goalkeeper Chris Harker in September 1963, Hayes suffered severe knee ligament damage, an injury that kept him out of first team action for 17 months. He played just two more times for City before a move to Barnsley in June 1965. His 52 goals in 142 reserve games for the club is also worthy of high praise.

After 25 League games at Barnsley, Hayes was transferred to Wigan Athletic before finishing his career as player-manager with non-League side Lancaster City. In later years Hayes was employed by a finance company before eventually opening his own greengrocery business in Bolton.

Joe Hayes, a much-loved and popular player (not to mention prolific goalscorer) at Maine Road, lost his battle with cancer in February 1999 when aged just 63.

Maine Road career

364 games   152 goals

Alex Herd – like father, like son

LESS than three months after joining City from Hamilton Academical, Alex Herd was playing in an FA Cup Final at Wembley.

After signing for the Blues on 1 February 1933, he was an ever-present for the rest of the season, playing 16 times in the League and four in the Cup. Considering he was new to not only his teammates but also to English football, his goalscoring return of seven in those games (all in the League) is a fine one. His arrival in Manchester coincided with an upsurge in City's fortunes. The club finished 16th in his debut season, fifth and fourth in the next two. The fast thinking (and running) inside-forward proved to be a great team player, one who linked the defence with the attack as well as being more than capable of scoring himself. The partnership of Herd, Brook and Tilson up front overcame the disappointment of the Blues' defeat by Everton in that 1933 FA Cup Final and steered City through to Wembley again 12 months later, this time to success against Portsmouth. Herd and Tilson joint topped the scoring charts that particular season (21 goals each) although Herd did score five more in League games. Manager Wilf Wild obviously knew he'd bought 'a good 'un', what he couldn't have known at the time though was he'd be 'a good 'un' for 15 years at Maine Road.

If the Blues had already enjoyed good runs in both League and Cup, things got even better in 1937. City were now able to boast the mercurial talents of Irishman Peter Doherty in an already potent attack, one that scored 107 goals, and won the First Division title. Herd's personal contribution was 15. And yet, despite all this continued firepower, inexplicably (and despite scoring more goals than any other team in the division) they were relegated next time out.

When war was declared in September 1939 Herd joined the army yet still found time to turn out in 90 wartime games for City. Once again his scoring achievements are more than worthy of a mention; his 60 successful strikes are beaten only by James Currier (with 84) and equalled by Doherty. Like many other players he lost arguably some of his best playing years to the war. By the time the League started again in August 1946 he was 35, although he was still capable of playing in 28 League games, his 11 goals helping the Blues towards lifting the Second Division championship. As with Stuart Pearce some 56 years later, it seemed the perfect finale to a fine career. For all his obvious talent and ability it seems difficult to understand quite why he was never chosen to represent his country. The nearest he came was being selected for the Scottish FA and even that honour fell during the war.

On 11 March 1948 he moved to Stockport County on a free transfer where he played more than 100 times in three seasons before retiring in 1951. He scored 35 times for the Edgeley Park side, in itself a remarkable achievement when he was almost 40. Also at Stockport at the time was Herd's son David, a man who would himself go on to to FA Cup Final success, this time with Manchester United. Remarkably both father and son lined up in the same Stockport side during a game against Hartlepool United in Herd's last season in the game.

Alex Herd was born in the small Scottish Border village of Bowhill on 8 November 1911. He died in his adopted Manchester in 1982 aged 70.

Maine Road career

288 appearances   125 goals   (not including wartime games)

George Heslop – well worth the wait

ACCORDING to Malcolm Allison, George Heslop signed for City on "the instalment plan of about £1,000 a month".

It was September 1965, just a few weeks after Allison had joined forces with Joe Mercer to begin about their remarkable upheaval of the club. With the Blues having already signed Mike Summerbee and Stan Horne, money was even tighter than usual as City began their Second Division championship challenge.

By the time he signed for City, Heslop was a player with six years professional experience, split evenly between Newcastle United (his first club) and Everton. However he failed to really establish himself at either club, playing a combined total of just 37 League games. His biggest stumbling block at Goodison Park was the presence of England centre-half Brian Labone. Allison watched him play a few times in Central League games and decided that, as understudy to the international, he must be capable of doing a job and he could do that job at Maine Road.

Born in Wallsend in July 1940, Heslop eventually cost £20,000 but gave the Blues' defence the required stability it had needed for some time. A powerfully built man, strong in the tackle and a good header of the ball, his debut came in a 3-3 draw at Norwich. A virtual ever-present for the rest of the season he was a pivotal figure in a side that clinched the Second Division. In one season with City his appearances totalled 34 in the League; just three less than his previous six had produced.

It was the same story in 1966-67, the season of consolidation in Division One. Heslop was one of seven players who took part in more than 40 games as Mercer and Allison's side began to take shape.

By the end of the following season the Blues had won the First Division title and the regular team could be rattled off by football supporters the length and breadth of the country. It was a team that was loved by (almost) everyone who saw them play. Only Tony Book, with 50 appearances, made more appearances than Heslop, and that was by just one. The half-back line of Doyle, Heslop and Oakes, had more than a touch of skill and professionalism about it. This was also the season that Heslop scored his one and only League goal in City's first team. And what a time he chose to score it.

With both Manchester clubs fighting for top spot, City travelled to Old Trafford on 27 March 1968, for one of the greatest Wednesday nights in 'derby' history. In the 57th minute Heslop's head met Tony Coleman's free-kick to give City a 2-1 lead in front of a silenced Stretford End. It was his 103rd League game, and when Francis Lee converted a penalty a few minutes later, the Blues had finally laid the red ghost. City would lose just one of the next 13 League 'derbies'. It was Heslop's header that started a six-year run of superiority.

Despite missing one League game of the championship season, Heslop's appearances for City began to be limited next time out owing the emergence of Tommy Booth. He started the season as captain for the 6-1 Charity Shield win against West Bromwich Albion at Maine Road but played in only four games (one of those as a substitute) from November onwards. Even though Booth would eventually become the first choice centre-half, Heslop was still a much-valued member of a relative small squad and was still respected highly enough to be included in the League Cup and European Cup-winners' Cup Finals of 1970. A rainy night in the Prater Stadium in Vienna was a long way from his schoolboy days with Dudley Welfare.

On Christmas Eve 1971 he moved to South Africa and joined Cape Town City for an eight-month loan period. In August 1972 his career at Maine Road ended completely when he signed for Fourth Division Bury.

Following a brief spell as manager of Northwich, Heslop retired from the game and began a new life in the licensed trade, one of his pubs being the renamed City Gates Hotel on Hyde Road, a pub that had once been a focal point in the club's formative days. In more recent times he's been employed as a social worker on the Fylde Coast but still retains connections with Manchester as his son Christopher runs his own chiropractic clinic in Urmston.

George Heslop was a key member of the great Mercer-Allison sides, particularly in the first four years of their partnership. Not one of the 'glamourous stars' of the late 1960s, the abundance of attack minded players in front of him would have had a more difficult time had Heslop not been behind them marshalling a well-organised defence.

Maine Road career
198-6 appearances   3 goals

Andy Hinchcliffe – a beautiful cross-field ball

ANY City fan who had the good fortune to be at Maine Road for the famous 5-1 thrashing of Alex Ferguson's multi-million pound Manchester United in September 1989 can remember each and every one of those goals in the most minute of details. Even though they were all 'great' perhaps the best one was the last, ironically enough scored by a defender.

Andy Hinchcliffe was the player who had the marvellous fortune to be scorer of that famous fifth goal. When David White's superb first-time cross was met on the run by Hinchcliffe's bullet header, it was the final humiliation for the Reds' supporters, many of whom had begun to leave their seats before the referee had blown his whistle to restart the game. Hinchcliffe's five-fingered salute to the remaining devastated United fans only endeared himself even more to the banks of joyous Blues on the Kippax.

A locally-born player, Hinchcliffe first came to prominence as member of the richly talented and successful City youth team of 1986. As a 16-year-old he'd signed apprentice forms less than 12 months earlier, his tackling and powerful left foot already showing great promise for the future. In the same year as City's success in the Youth Cup, Hinchcliffe became a regular in the reserve team with his performances receiving glowing praise from coach Tony Book. Knowing a fair bit himself about the necessary qualities required to become a proficient full-back, Book was already tipping the young player for a career in the first team and full international honours. As time went on he'd be proved right on both points.

Manager Mel Machin agreed wholeheartedly with Book's observations and gave Hinchcliffe (despite a back problem) his senior debut in the opening game of the 1987-88 season, a 2-1 win at home to Plymouth Argyle. He played a remarkable 55 times in his debut season (including all bar two of the 44 League games), scoring four times, interestingly enough one in each of the four different competitions he played in. Only his former youth team colleague Steve Redmond, with 58 appearances, played in more games. He bettered his scoring record next time out with five successes in 43-2 outings. This was the memorable 1988-89 season when Trevor Morley's equaliser in the dying minutes at Bradford earned the Blues promotion to the First Division.

Scoring is not the number one priority for a full-back. His job is to break up the opposition attacks and distribute the ball to his own midfielders and attackers. This was a task Hinchcliffe was more than up to. He also had his own particular forte; that was the long distance cross-field pass, one that benefited the rampaging David White regularly. His other specialty was the inswinging corner, his powerfully hit centres causing numerous problems for goalkeepers and defenders alike.

By the end of the 1989-90 season (one in which he'd appeared for England's Under-21 side) Hinchcliffe had just turned 21, had played more than 130 times for the Blues and had been a regular for three seasons. It seemed as though he had many years ahead of him at Maine Road but the recently appointed Howard Kendall felt differently. He thought another tough-tackling left-back (coincidentally another Everton player) Neil Pointon was a better bet and so a swap deal valued at £600,000 was arranged between the two clubs. Not surprisingly City fans were hugely surprised by the departure of such a highly thought of player. The fact that Pointon (like several before him) had come from Goodison Park did little to calm the frustrated Blues' followers.

Hinchcliffe stayed at Goodison Park for seven and a half years, was part of their FA Cup winning team in 1995 and, as predicted, played for England. Pointon on the other hand, good player though he was, stayed for two years before being sold to Oldham Athletic. The sale of Andy Hinchcliffe was perhaps not the greatest bit of business the club ever did.

In January 1998 Hinchcliffe joined Sheffield Wednesday, a club he was still at in 2002 when a long-term knee injury finally caused his retirement from the game.

He undoubtedly liked playing against the allegedly more illustrious neighbours from Old Trafford. Having beaten them to clinch the Youth Cup in 1986, he scored against them in the 5-1 and as an Everton player was victorious over them at Wembley. It's a pity he wasn't given the chance to stay at Maine Road even longer in the hope he might have inflicted some more misfortune on them.

Maine Road career
134-5 appearances   11 goals

Tommy Hutchison – nice while it lasted

IN October 1980, City were bottom of the First Division and without a win in their first 11 games. In May the following year they were playing in the 100th FA Cup Final and had climbed to twelfth place, a position of mid-table security and one that fans thought impossible just a few months earlier.

One reason for this upturn in both form and stability was the change of manager, from Malcolm Allison and Tony Book to the former Norwich boss John Bond. Perhaps the major reason though was the arrival of three players – all within the space of a few days at the end of October. The players concerned were Gerry Gow, a no-nonsense midfielder from Bristol City, full-back Bobby McDonald and his Coventry teammate, winger Tommy Hutchison. All three brought with them a vast amount of experience (over 1,000 League games between them up to that point), something that was lacking at Maine Road at the time.

Cardenden-born Hutchison had recently celebrated his 33rd birthday when he arrived at Maine Road, although he was by no means at the end of his playing career. It was a career that had started back in the early 1960s at Alloa, progressing to Blackpool in 1968. Capped for Scotland at Under-21 and full level, Hutchison's twisting and turning runs along the wings at Bloomfield Road made him a firm favourite with the Blackpool fans for four years before a move to Coventry in October 1972. Unquestionably he had his best years at Coventry.

In a team that regularly toyed with relegation, Hutchison was probably the most skilful player. His close control made it very difficult for defenders to take the ball from him and he provided a seemingly endless supply of crosses to his waiting (but not always clinical) teammates.

He'd played more than 300 League games for Coventry by the time Bond offered him the position at Maine Road. Hutchison's debut (alongside McDonald) was in the 2-1 home win against Brighton three days after putting pen to paper. It was only the Blues' second League win of the season but started a run of 12 games up until Christmas in which City lost just twice.

They continued this fine form when the FA Cup came into view in January. By the time they reached Wembley in May to face Tottenham, Hutchison had already become a crucial part of City's style of play. He missed only a handful of League games and played in every round of the Cup run, one in which the by now thoroughly entertaining Blues had scored 17 times. Hutchison himself provided the 18th.

In the 29th minute of the Final he flung himself almost horizontally to send a terrific diving header past Aleksic in the Spurs goal. His next header goalwards had drastic consequences for his team. Whilst defending a Glenn Hoddle free-kick, Hutchison overheard the future England manager's plans to bend it round the wall and dropped out of the defensive line accordingly. True to his word Hoddle curled the ball, Hutchison's head met it on the full and the ball flew past a despairing Joe Corrigan who was going in the opposite direction. It was a desperately unlucky way to have the Cup taken away from them. Five days later City failed to cope with the Argentinean Ricardo Villa and their chances of Wembley glory had gone. No blame at all can be apportioned to Hutchison, indeed had it not been for his contribution throughout the season, the Blues would never have been given the chance in the first place.

His appearances were limited to the first half of the following season, 1981-82, and he left the club in July to play for the Hong Kong side Bulova. On his return to England in August 1983 he joined Burnley, the start of a two-year spell in which he took part in over 100 games. When he signed for the soon to be relegated Third Division side Swansea in the 1985 close season, he was nearly 38 but still not finished as a player. That came amazingly five years and 178 League games later when he was 43, a tribute to way Hutchison looked after himself as well as his always-high levels of fitness.

Although Hutchison was only at Maine Road for two seasons he left its supporters with many happy memories. Even today he is still a more than welcome visitor to the ground and to various Supporters' Club meetings. It was such a shame that he only wore the Manchester sky-blue in the latter part of his playing days. Had it worn it throughout his prime, he would have left the fans with considerably many more happy memories.

Maine Road appearances
57-3 appearances   5 goals

Tommy Johnson – a record that may never be broken

ALTHOUGH Shaun Goater came closer than most in the 2001-02 season, the amazing goalscoring feats of Thomas Clark Fisher Johnson ('Tosh' to his friends and teammates) are still intact after more than 70 years.

Back in 1928-29, Johnson's penultimate season with City, he scored a remarkable 38 goals in 39 League appearances. These included a hat-trick against Bolton Wanderers and an astonishing five in a 6-2 win at Everton. The management at Goodison Park would file away Johnson's achievements that day in their collective memory banks for future reference.

He was personally responsible for more than a third of the Blues' output that particular season (the team scored an impressive 95 in the League) with his nearest rival, Eric Brook, being the small matter of 24 strikes behind him. Brook would have the last laugh though, eventually becoming the club's all-time leading scorer with Johnson in second place. However it was only Brook's apparent penchant for scoring in the FA Cup that made the difference; both men scored an identical 158 times in League games.

Born in August 1901 in Dalton-in-Furness, Johnson started out his career with the splendidly named local side Dalton Casuals. With a scoring record like Johnson's it seems as though he was far from his team description when it came to chances in front of goal. In February 1919 then City captain Eli Fletcher had seen Johnson play a few times and strongly recommended him to manager Ernest Mangnall. Rumour has it that Fletcher was so insistent Johnson came to Hyde Road that he threatened to resign if a deal could not be done. Fortunately for Fletcher and for the club, a deal was done, and Johnson embarked on a career with City lasting 11 years and more than 350 games. During that time he'd be promoted (as champions), relegated, finish a runner-up in Division One, be on the losing side in an FA Cup Final and be capped for England.

His first appearance for City was against Blackburn Rovers in a Lancashire Section game in the same month as his arrival at Hyde Road. Johnson scored in that 5-1 win, two weeks later his hat-trick in a 6-1 win against Port Vale only confirmed Fletcher's first impressions were right on the mark. When the full League programme commenced again the next season (1919-20, after World War One) Johnson could only manage 10 first-team appearances in the League as Messrs. Barnes and Browell continued their most prolific double act. Johnson though was yet to reach his 20th birthday; he still had a lot of time ahead of him.

Bu the end of the 1922-23 season, City's last at Hyde Road, Johnson had gradually taken over from Browell as Barnes' striking partner. His tally of 15 goals that season was exactly the same as his combined efforts for the previous three years.

As the Blues progressed towards Wembley for the first time in 1926, Johnson found the net in both the third and sixth rounds, his efforts climaxing in the quarter-final with a hat-trick against Clapton Orient. A season that had certainly had its highs (including a 6-1 victory at Old Trafford – Johnson's header made it 4-0) was ultimately a disappointing one as the Blues lost to Bolton in the FA Cup Final and then suffered relegation a few days later.

Two years later City were back in the top flight after winning the Second Division title by two points from second-placed Leeds United. Johnson was joint top scorer with Frank Roberts (20 goals each), was an established first-team player, hugely popular with the supporters of the day and about to begin his record-breaking season.

On 5 March 1930 the Blues appeared to have made a grave error of judgement when they sold the productive Johnson to Everton for £8,500. He was still only 29 and when he won successive Second and First Division championship medals (in his first two seasons) on Merseyside it seemed as though there was some truth in the disappointed City fans anger. At Goodison, Johnson partnered arguably the greatest-ever goalscorer in British football, Dixie Dean, a strikeforce that took Everton to Wembley in 1933 and, a further irony, victory over Manchester City.

After leaving Everton, Johnson joined rivals Liverpool for one season before ending his playing days in the non-League colours of Darwen. By the time he'd retired he'd won every domestic honour available to him. With players being paid the proverbial 'peanuts' back then, these were justifiable rewards for a man whose goals thrilled supporters in both Manchester and Liverpool.

He was 71 years of age when he passed away in Manchester's Monsall Hospital in January 1973.

Hyde Road-Maine Road career

354 appearances   166 goals

Bobby Johnstone – part of Wembley folklore

WHATEVER he lacked in inches, there was no doubting Selkirk-born Bobby Johnstone's stature as a professional footballer. In a Maine Road career spanning four and a half years, the diminutive Scottish international with a shrewd footballing brain became a hugely popular player with the City supporters.

Before joining City he had already proved himself north of the border with Hibernian, his first professional club. As a member of a renowned forward line – The Famous Five – Johnstone had won three Scottish championships, been runner-up on three other occasions and had been capped 13 times by the time he arrived at Maine Road on 2 March 1955. His fee was £20,700; a fairly high sum at the time but manager Les McDowall knew what a good player Johnstone was. Within a few short weeks, so too would the Blues fans standing on the terraces.

Injuries to Johnny Hart and Roy Clarke gave Johnstone his debut just two weeks later (and probably a little earlier than even McDowall thought) in a 4-2 win against Bolton Wanderers. The equally diminutive Joe Hayes was so delighted with having someone else alongside of him who caused him little neck discomfort, that he celebrated the Scot's arrival with a hat-trick.

Less than two months after his debut, Johnstone was playing in an FA Cup Final at Wembley. For all his successes in the League in Scotland, he'd never made it to a Scottish FA Cup Final. Although the wait was over, he would be disappointed with his first one; 10-men City lost 3-1 to Newcastle United. Johnstone scored City's goal with a diving header, admitted later he should have scored a second but soon put all footballing thoughts out of his head and concentrated the rest of the summer on his second sporting love, cricket. He continued to play league cricket in and around his adopted Oldham until after his 50th birthday. Not surprisingly because of his passion for the summer game, Johnstone became great friends with his City teammate and Lancashire player Jack Dyson.

On 2 January 1956 Johnstone scored his first hat-trick for City in a 4-1 win against Portsmouth at Maine Road. Ken Barnes is quoted as remembering Johnstone had celebrated the New Year with far too much gusto (as is the way for the majority of Scots) and arrived for the game "stinking of booze". After the game – and Johnstone's hat-trick of headers – Barnes suggested he should prepare every week in the same way!

City's next venture into the FA Cup took them back to Wembley, this time with more success. Johnstone's personal contribution to the Cup run consisted of goals against Blackpool in the third round, Everton in the sixth round and another header was enough to finish Tottenham in the semi-final. Arguably though he saved the best until last; the Final itself. Following Trautmann's long clearance and Dyson's flick, Johnstone shrugged off the challenges of two Birmingham defenders before scoring City's third – and decisive – goal. His 67th-minute strike meant he'd become the first player ever to score in successive FA Cup Finals.

Next time out, the 1956-57 season, proved Johnstone's most productive. His 19 goals in all competitions (making him top scorer) came thanks to League hat-tricks against Everton and Cardiff City (the last of his City career) and he scored three goals for the club in their defence of the FA Cup. Two of his three goals were scored at Maine Road in the third-round replay with Newcastle in January. City led 3-0 at half-time only to lose an amazing game 5-4 and with it their chances of retaining the Cup.

Johnstone won four Scottish caps whilst with City and played for Great Britain against the Rest of Europe in 1955. His teammates that day included some of the greatest British players of all time. Stanley Matthews, Danny Blanchflower and John Charles give some indication of just how good a player Bobby Johnstone was and just what esteem he was held in.

By September 1959 Johnstone had become disillusioned with life at Maine Road. Having just avoided relegation in the very last game of the previous season, by his own admittance, Johnstone confessed to being fed up with the constant changes and was happy to rejoin Hibs for a £3,000 fee. After a year back in Scotland, Johnstone joined Oldham Athletic, no doubt missing his friends as well as his beloved cricket.

Leaving football in 1965, Johnstone, then 36, worked firstly in engineering and then at Smithfield Market in Manchester. He spent his early retirement in Hollinwood before returning to Scotland in the mid-1990s. But he missed Manchester and came back in 1999. Two years later, on 22 August 2001, he passed away, aged 71.

Maine Road career

139 appearances   51 goals

Billy Lot Jones – tricky, erratic and loyal

THE name Billy Meredith will be forever synonymous with Welsh football and Manchester City in the early years of the last century. And quite rightly so; he was a legend in the game and one of its most famous figures.

Yet there was another Welshman, one who was arguably as important to both club and country but who never quite achieved Meredith's 'superstar' status. That man was Billy Lot Jones, a man who was born in the same north Wales town as Meredith (Chirk, in Denbighshire, just a few hundreds yards from the border with Shropshire), and one who would play more than 300 times for City and win 20 caps in what was at the time, a very strong Welsh national side.

Jones was a player who liked to play up front; any position would do for this highly-skilled footballer, just as long as he didn't have to defend too much. During his 16 years with City he played in every attacking position and was always capable of setting off on a mazy, dribbling run from anywhere on the pitch. If he had one drawback – arguably a major one for a player who liked to attack so much – it was his poor finishing. One contemporary journalist described him as "a remarkably tricky footballer with one of the worst shots I've ever seen". Unfortunately over the years, Jones apparent ineptitude has reared its head time and time again in future generations of City players!

He joined the Hyde Road side on 19 January 1903 from Rushton Druids but had to wait until the following April for his debut in the first team, a 2-1 defeat at the hands of West Bromwich Albion. Jones scored on his debut, a game that proved to be his one and only that season.

His big break at the club came after the alleged bribery scandal of 1905. In April that year with the Blues pushing hard for the championship, they needed maximum points from their trip to Villa Park on the last day of the season. After the Blues had lost the bad tempered game 3-2, the Villa captain Alec Leake claimed Billy Meredith had offered him a bribe in an attempt the throw the game, thereby increasing City's chances of clinching the title for the first time. The ensuing investigations by the FA led eventually to 17 players (including Meredith) and four members of the management being suspended. Jones himself played in the game at Villa Park but was cleared of any apparent wrongdoing.

Playing alongside newcomers, Blair and Conlin, Jones now began to play possibly the best football of his career, forming a more than useful partnership with the two Jimmy's on City's left-hand side. The necessary shake-up also provided Jones with the opportunity to captain the side, a position he held for seven seasons from 1908-09. His first season in charge showed a drop of 16 places from the previous campaign. Having finished a highly creditable third in 1907-08, City were now 19th and with only 20 teams in the division it meant relegation. The next season proved much better for Jones and for City.

After just one season in the Second Division the Blues won promotion, finishing as champions by a single point from their Lancashire neighbours Oldham Athletic. Along with George Dorsett, Jones scored 14 times to jointly head the scoring charts; it proved to be the only occasion the Welshman achieved this feat.

In 1908 the club rewarded him with the gate receipts from a game with Middlesbrough. Jones was delighted when the final figure was calculated as he was £835 better off. He knew immediately what to do with the money. He gave all of it to his former teammate and great friend Meredith who had fallen on hard times when his sports shop was ruined by fire. Jones was a remarkable team man even off the pitch.

He continued to play at Hyde Road throughout World War One, although his appearances (37 in total) did become fewer and fewer as the hostilities continued. In August 1919, just a few weeks before the return of League football, the 37-year-old Jones moved to Southend. After spells with Aberdare, Wrexham and Oswestry, he finished his footballing days with his home-town club Chirk. Although he was well into his 40s when he finished playing (a remarkable achievement in those pioneering sports medicine days) he would unfortunately not endure a long and happy retirement.

Billy Lot Jones, the owner of a successful chain of grocery stores in Chirk, died in the town on 13 July 1941 at the relatively young age of 59.

Hyde Road career

302 appearances   74 goals   not including wartime games

Bobby Kennedy – "Well, it's his own fault!"

WHEN you share the same name as a world famous person, no matter what sort of business you are in, your workmates are bound to ridicule you.

City's Motherwell-born Bobby Kennedy, a man who played for the Blues in the dark days of the early 1960s right the way through to just a few months before the 1969 FA Cup Final success, was of course no different. Possibly by working constantly amongst 20 or 30 athletic males, he was the subject of mickey-taking more than most. Having the same name as US Senator Robert Kennedy, a major player on the world political stage at the time, City's version was the victim of a wonderful piece of confusion on a summer tour to North America in 1968. This time though, it was the Blues' chairman Albert Alexander who unwittingly instigated perhaps the biggest session of mickey-taking of all.

City had travelled across the Atlantic as champions of England, taking part in a series of exhibition games in Canada, the United States and (supposedly) Mexico. Because of the number of games to be played in such a short period of time, Joe Mercer had insisted on a 10 o'clock curfew for all his players. Shortly before retiring for bed himself one night, Mercer switched on the television and caught the midnight news. The major story was the shooting of (Senator) Bobby Kennedy. Eager to convey the news to his chairman, Mercer immediately rang Mr. Alexander. The chairman's reply has gone into City folklore; "Well, it's his own fault. He shouldn't have been out so late at night!"

The footballing Kennedy was already a Scottish Under-23 international by the time he signed for the Blues from Kilmarnock on 20 July 1961, the same week as Peter Dobing arrived from Blackburn Rovers. The fee of £45,000 was a British record for a wing-half but it proved to be money very well spent.

Having been paid for by the sale of Denis Law to Torino, both newcomers made their debuts on the opening day of the 1961-62 season, a 3-1 home win against Leicester. Kennedy marked his debut not only with a highly competent performance but also with a goal, the first of six he scored in the League that year. He also played in every game and missed just one of the next campaign. He was equally at home at either right-back or right-half and developed a reputation as being a strong tackler, the owner of a fierce shot (as proved on his debut) and a more than useful long-throw, certainly the longest at the club in those days.

As all Blues' followers know, the arrival of Mercer and Allison in the summer of 1965 revitalised the struggling City side. Having played through some extremely disappointing seasons, Kennedy was rewarded for his efforts with a Second Division championship medal in 1966. It was the first winners' medal he'd collected in a professional career that had so far lasted nine years. He'd come close with Kilmarnock twice in the Scottish FA Cup and had been a runner-up in the League. Having also recovered from a serious long-term illness during his days in Scotland, it did seem as though he was due something. Unfortunately for the likeable Scot, Mercer and Allison were nurturing the talents of home-grown youngsters such as Mike Doyle, Glyn Pardoe and Alan Oakes, not to mention bringing in Tony Book from Plymouth. All these players were contenders for the positions Kennedy played in and consequently he found his opportunities limited.

He hardly figured at all in the First Division championship season of 1967-68 (4-2 appearances) and played just 10 times in 1968-69, mainly as cover for the injured Book. His last game for the Blues was on 23 November 1968, a 5-1 win against West Bromwich Albion.

In March the following year he left Maine Road to become player-manager at Grimsby. The Blues received £10,000 for Kennedy, a figure that The Mariners must surely have struggled to come up with, languishing as they were at the bottom of Division Four. Kennedy's arrival at Blundell Park failed to prevent an application for re-election and things faired only marginally better over the next two years, resulting in his dismissal in May 1971. After a brief flirtation with Irish side Drogheda, Kennedy spent the next seven years at Bradford City, originally developing a much-praised youth policy and eventually managing the first team. His last job in the game was coaching for a short time with Jim Smith's Blackburn in the early part of 1978.

Away from football, Bobby Kennedy has been in the clothing trade for the last 20 years, living for a long time near Longford Park in Stretford. He currently owns a high-class ladies' fashion shop in Hebden Bridge and plays a bit of golf; when his troublesome knee allows.

....

Maine Road career
251-3 appearances   9 goals

Georgiou Kinkladze – jewel in a tarnished crown

CITY fans who had the pleasure to witness at first hand the mercurial talents of the Georgian international Georgi Kinkladze will still remember with great affection the number of times his individual brilliance alone brightened up an otherwise lacklustre team performance.

There was no questioning his obvious footballing talents. What did seem to be in question at times however was his commitment to the cause. For three years in the mid-1990s, City sides (with not one single player coming anywhere near to Kinkladze as a footballer) relied on him, and him alone, to pull them out of difficult situations. Regretfully of course, this was just not possible and even with Kinkladze in the side, the Blues were relegated twice during his three seasons at Maine Road. In 2002, he would suffer the same fate again, this time with Derby County.

Kinkladze was born in Tblisi, Georgia on 6 November 1973. As a boy he supported the local side, Dynamo, but would eventually progress through the junior ranks of rivals FC Mrettebi to become the star of their first team. By the early part of 1995, chairman Francis Lee began to hear glowing reports on the player now with Dynamo and continued to monitor his progress over a six-month period. When Kinkladze scored a brilliant goal against Wales at Cardiff, Lee knew it was the time to act. Even without a manager, Lee knew Kinkladze would be a tremendous asset to the club and finalised a £2 million deal on 14 July 1995, the same day as new manager Alan Ball also arrived at Maine Road. When Ball saw him for the first time he said, "I think we might have just found ourselves a gem." After Kinkladze's debut against Tottenham on 19 August, City fans knew immediately what the former World Cup winner meant.

From the outset Kinkladze proved to be an entertainer and within a few short weeks had risen beyond the heights of mere popularity with the fans to those of an idol. Undoubtedly the most skilful and talented footballer City fans had seen in a long, long time, Kinkladze was a naturally gifted player, one who could split defences open with his accurate passing as well as having remarkably quick feet. Despite standing at just 5ft 8ins tall, he proved to be a strong, robust player and one who proved virtually unstoppable when in full flow with the ball.

Perhaps his greatest performance in City's colours came in a 4-1 win at Oxford in 1997. Not content with scoring twice himself, he single-handedly destroyed the home side with a breath-taking display, one that showed virtually every trick in his repertoire. If that was his greatest overall performance then he most certainly saved his best two goals for Maine Road. Against Southampton in March 1996, the culmination of a brilliant, mazy 40-yard run was a delightful chip over the advancing Dave Beasant in goal, whilst in the FA Cup the following season, West Ham suffered a similar fate, although in the end the Londoners went on to win the tie 2-1.

Although the Blues were undoubtedly a struggling side during Kinkladze's time, he proved his loyalty by agreeing a new three-year deal at Francis Lee's house on Cup Final day 1997, one that, up to that point, made him City's highest paid player of all time. Whatever his weekly salary was, had he asked for double, every City fan would have told Lee to pay it.

With 15 games left and City seemingly unable to prevent a slide into Division Two (technically Three), Joe Royle took over in February 1998. Under the circumstances, Royle felt a more battling style was called for and as a result Kinkladze's appearances became limited. Unfortunately Royle was unable to prevent the dreaded relegation, causing fans to suggest that had he played Kinkladze more, City would have been safe although in Royle's defence there seems to be little evidence to suggest that would have been the case.

Not surprisingly (although certainly disappointingly) Kinkladze joined Ajax of Amsterdam in the summer shortly after relegation, his transfer fee of £4,925,000 being the most City have ever received for a player. He was played as a right-winger in Holland, a position he was not used to and consequently his form suffered. After a disappointing 10 games in 15 months, Kinkladze began a loan period back in England with Derby County, one that became permanent (thanks to £3 million) in April 2000. Whist at Maine Road Kinkladze was capped 17 times for Georgia and was voted City's Player of the Year in two successive seasons. With both City and Derby, he found himself a luxury that neither side at the time could afford. Had he had the good fortune to play under Kevin Keegan, only speculation can say things might have been different.

Maine Road career

120-1 appearances   22 goals

Paul Lake – a loss to the nation

DENTON-BORN Paul Lake was one of the most naturally-gifted and talented footballers ever to wear the colours of Manchester City. He was also a desperately unlucky one. The former England Under-21 and B international was still two months short of his 22nd birthday when a knee injury effectively finished his career.

Having played for local side Blue Star, Lake first came to prominence as an influential member of City's FA Youth Cup-winning side in 1986. A versatile player who could (and did) play literally anywhere, it would be on the left-hand side of midfield where he'd turn in his best performances for the Blues. He made his senior debut in January 1987 in a goalless draw at Wimbledon, going on to play in two more games that season (both times he was substituted) before becoming a regular starter in 1987-88.

In that Second Division season (the Blues had been relegated in his debut one) Lake played a part in 43 games, wearing nine different shirts along the way. Manager Mel Machin also gave chances to the bulk of that 1986 youth team and for a while at least, the long-term future of the club looked rosy. In September 1988 he won the first of his six England Under-21 caps in a game against Denmark. His performances at this level prompted glowing praise from England manager Bobby Robson who predicted great things for Lake in the future as well as pencilling him in for his provisional 1990 World Cup squad. Also in 1988 he was voted the club's Young Player of the Year.

In March 1989 a near tragedy almost befell him. Defending a Leicester corner in a game at Maine Road he was the accidental victim of a sickening clash of heads with the opposition's Paul Ramsey. Lake collapsed to the floor, began convulsing and swallowed his tongue. Had it not been for the swift reactions of physiotherapist Roy Bailey, Lake would in all probability have lost his life.

Promotion back to the First Division followed in May that year thereby giving Lake the opportunity to display his outstanding talents at the highest level. By now his confidence had grown to such a degree that he began almost single-handedly to control games from the middle of the park. In professional language, he had a great 'engine', was strong in the tackle, good in the air and was a fine passer of the ball. All the qualities required to make a top-class midfielder, Paul Lake had in abundance. Fans and players alike looked to Lake to lead by example, something he was always capable of doing.

Perhaps his finest all-round performance in a blue shirt came on 23 September 1989 when he was outstanding as City's youngsters outplayed the multi-million pound Manchester United in the famous 5-1 game.

However Lake's life took an awful turn for the worse 12 months later. Having apparently secured his future with the club after negotiating a new five-year contract, he injured his knee in an innocuous challenge with Aston Villa's Tony Cascarino just three games into the new season. The recently installed captain underwent two complicated operations and didn't play again for two years. On 19 August 1992, in only his second game back, Lake collapsed during the 2-0 defeat at Middlesbrough. This time the injury was worse; he'd damaged his cruciate knee ligaments. Apart from a brief showing to kick-off his testimonial game against Manchester United five years later, it was his last appearance for the Blues.

After years of long and lonely struggling, Lake was finally forced to retire in 1996. The combined knee injuries robbed City and England of the services of a marvellous footballer, one who could easily have given service to both club and country for another decade. If there was any consolation to come out of Lake's misfortunes it was the fact that he now knows so much about sports injuries and the workings of the human body, it has giving him a tremendous grounding in his new career as a physiotherapist.

Howard Kendall once described Lake as "the most talented footballer I ever worked with." When you take Kendall's career and experience into account, it gives you some idea of Lake's capabilities. It was such a tragedy that injuries limited him to a little over three full seasons appearances with City.

Maine Road career
130-4 appearances   11 goals

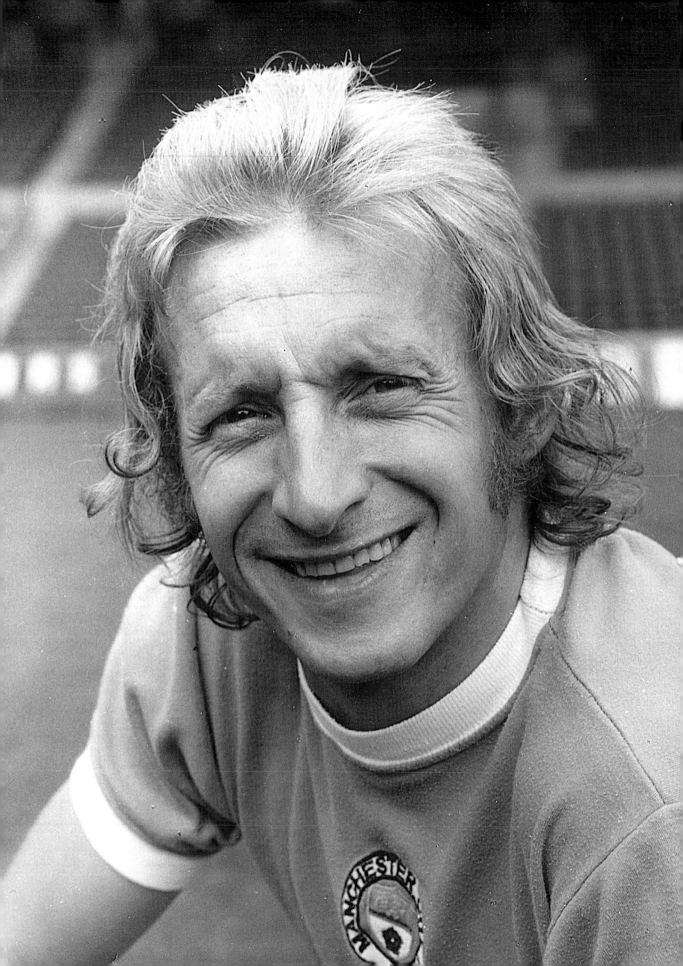

Denis Law – "Denis has done it!"

IF Francis Lee will be forever remembered as a great player with Manchester City, but also played a bit for Derby County, then the same could almost be said about Denis Law.

Law will be always be remembered as the 'King' at Old Trafford, and quite rightly so, having played more than 300 League games in the red of United over a 10-year period, scoring the best part of 200 times. Yet both before and after he was a Red, he was most certainly a Blue, and even if his combined career at Maine Road falls quite a way short of his achievements at Old Trafford, he still provided City supporters with a few memorable moments.

Fortunately for both sets of Manchester football supporters it was no less a person than the great Bill Shankly who first spotted Law's potential in English football. It was whilst managing Huddersfield Town that Shankly gave a trial to a small, scrawny 16-year-old Aberdeen lad with bad eyesight. His initial, outward appearance disguised what lay beneath; namely an incredibly gifted, natural goalscorer, the like of which would cost the economy of a small country in today's transfer market.

After 81 League games for Huddersfield (and 16 goals) Law was transferred to City on 15 March 1960 for a then British record fee of £55,000, making him Britain's first £50,000 player. Four days later he made his debut (and scored) in City's 4-3 defeat at Leeds. At the time Law's fee was enormous especially when taking into account City's lowly standing in the First Division. For the price manager Les McDowall paid for him another four of five players could have been bought, a much better way to spend the money, so the average man on the terrace thought. And yet McDowall, like Shankly, knew just what a talent Law was.

His first full season, 1960-61, saw him top the goalscoring charts with 23 in all competitions, a figure that would have been considerably higher had it not been for a bizarre fourth-round FA Cup tie at Luton. On a bog-like pitch, the home side took a two-goal lead only for Law's amazing 48-minute double hat-trick to put the Blues 6-2 up. Then, with a little over 20 minutes left and conditions worsening, the referee abandoned the game, ordering a replay four days later. In true City style, they lost the replay 3-1 with Law once again getting his name on the scoresheet. Unfortunately his six goals in the abandoned game are not eligible for the record books. Law was undoubtedly the star of a poor City side, a player who was obviously destined not to stay with the club for a long period of time.

On 13 July 1961 he was sold to the crack Italian side Torino for a fee of £110,000. Once again Law was a record breaker; now he'd become the first British player to be involved in a six-figure transfer. His stay in Italy equalled his short time at Maine Road; he lasted just one season before returning to Manchester. This time though he signed for Matt Busby at Old Trafford, the fee of £100,000 making United the first British club ever to spend that amount on a player.

There is no questioning Law had his best playing days with United. He also had the worst day of his footballing life on that same Old Trafford pitch. In July 1973 one of Britain's greatest ever goalscorers was surprisingly given a free transfer by Tommy Docherty. City boss Johnny Hart had no hesitation in snapping up the 33-year-old for one last Indian summer.

Law's second City debut came against Birmingham on the opening day of the season. Like his first 13 years before, he scored (this time twice) in City's 3-1 win. In March the following year he took his place at Wembley alongside, Summerbee, Bell, Lee and Marsh (one of the best forward-lines in the club's history) only to finish a loser as Wolves' somehow managed to snatch the League Cup from City's grasp. Just a few weeks after that Wembley disappointment, in the last game of the season, Law played for City in the Old Trafford 'derby'. With United fighting for their First Division lives, the ex-Red scored the only goal of the game, his now famous backheel effectively condemning his former club to the Second Division. Seconds after his goal, Law left the field almost in tears. It was his last kick in League football.

However it wasn't the last kick of his career. He'd played so well for the Blues throughout the season that he was chosen to represent Scotland in the World Cup finals held in West Germany. The fiercely patriotic Scot made two appearances, taking his tally of international caps to 55.

Nowadays Law is a highly sought after speaker on the after dinner circuit as well as being a respected television pundit. He is that rarest of men; one that is much-loved by both sets of Manchester football supporters. He was also a supreme goalscorer.

Maine Road career
80-2 appearances   38 goals

Francis Lee – final piece of the jigsaw

WHENEVER and wherever Francis Lee got the ball he only ever had one intention in mind; a shot on goal. With 148 successes, only five City players have ever managed to be more proficient at it than this supremely confident striker.

He began his career at Bolton Wanderers, where, as a 16-year-old he made his debut in League football. It was 15 November 1960, ironically in a game at Burnden Park against Manchester City. The home side won 3-1 with the debutant getting his name on the scoresheet against his future employers. It would be a further seven years before Lee made the short journey down the recently opened M62 motorway to join Joe Mercer and Malcolm Allison and their resurgent team.

At lot happened to Lee during that interim period. He played more than 200 games for Bolton, was capped by England Youth and laid the foundations for what turned out to be a hugely successful waste paper business. He was already showing the business acumen that would make him a multi-millionaire in later life. And yet, making money came a poor second to playing football. In June 1967 he was offered a new contract by Bolton, one that would raise his salary from £30 to £150 a week. Always ambitious, Lee refused to sign and by October that year he'd become City's record signing at £60,000.

His debut against Wolves began a run of 11 unbeaten League games and Lee was the vital spark needed to push the Blues to their first championship in 30 years. Alongside Summerbee, Bell and Young, he was an integral part of the City forward line that helped to bring success after success in a marvellous four-year period. In the same year City won the First Division title, Lee was recognised by Sir Alf Ramsey and won the first of his 27 England caps in a 1-1 draw with Bulgaria. Along with teammate Colin Bell, he would go on to represent his country in the Mexico World Cup of 1970.

Short, stocky and extremely powerful, he top scored in five out of six seasons from 1968-69, scoring some memorable goals along the way. He'd already scored the fourth (and decisive) goal in the championship decider at Newcastle and it was his (somewhat fortunate) penalty that clinched the European Cup-winners' Cup in a rain-soaked Vienna. In the successful League Cup run of 1970, he won, and then converted a late penalty to give City a slender one-goal advantage to take to Old Trafford for the second leg of the semi-final. Then, in the dying minutes of that game, he blasted an indirect free-kick through the Reds' defensive wall to give Mike Summerbee the opportunity to level the game and take City to Wembley. Although not scoring himself in the Final against West Bromwich Albion it is felt by many that this was his best game in City's colours. His most prolific season was 1971-72 when he scored 33 times in the League, including a record 13 penalties. This record earned him the nickname 'Lee One Pen', although analysis shows that not all these penalties were the result of fouls on Lee personally.

In August 1974, the 30-year-old Lee was unexpectedly sold to Dave Mackay's Derby County for £100,000. At the time Lee didn't want to leave and warned the club that they hadn't seen the last of him. And so it proved. Within four months of his departure he was back at Maine Road scoring a typical 30-yarder for his new club. It was a goal even the City fans applauded. He won his second championship medal with Derby before retiring at the end of the 1975-76 season, having played in exactly 500 (499 plus 1 substitute appearance) League games. In true Lee style he scored twice in the last two minutes of the Rams' 6-2 win at Ipswich in his last game.

After retiring from playing he concentrated on his waste paper business along with a more recent interest, training racehorses. And yet he still hadn't finished with football, and Manchester City in particular. In February 1994 following many months of negotiating and wave after wave of fans' support, Lee took over as chairman at Maine Road after Peter Swales had stepped down. Despite making many changes necessary to secure the club's financial footing, Lee's chairmanship coincided with a poor period on the playing side and he resigned from the position four years later. It should not be forgotten though that chairman Lee insisted on a strong youth set up at the club and was instrumental in the first stages of a proposed move to the (at the time unbuilt) Commonwealth Stadium, both crucial for the future development of the club.

The word 'great' is used far too often in connection with footballers. As far as Francis Lee was concerned, it's a perfect description.

Maine Road career

328-2 appearances   148 goals

Bill Leivers – another rock at the back

BOLSOVER-BORN Bill 'Don't' Leivers had a career in football that started in Chesterfield in 1950 and finished in Cambridge almost 40 years later.

He was a stalwart for the Blues for 10 seasons from the mid-1950s onwards, having signed from Third Division North Chesterfield on 27 November 1953 for £8,000. Standing 6ft 2ins tall and weighing in at 13st, Leivers was a powerfully built man, one who had the perfect physique for a centre-half, a position he'd played in for two seasons with Chesterfield.

His first appearance in City's colours was on the opening day of the 1954-55 season, a 5-0 defeat at Preston. It was not the most auspicious of starts for a country boy still acclimatising himself to life in the big city. His debut coincided with the introduction of the new Revie Plan and whilst that was persevered with, Leivers would have to wait until the following January for another opportunity in the first team. They were his only two appearances that season.

Leivers played at right-back in his first game and at centre-half in his second, an early indication of his future at Maine Road. He was equally at home in either position although he would ultimately have his greatest moments of success at right-back. After a handful of outings at centre-half covering for the injured Dave Ewing, Leivers took over Ken Branagan's spot at right-back just prior to Christmas 1955. He took his chance with both hands, staying in the side for the rest of the season, one that culminated in a Wembley victory over Birmingham. There was no questioning the defensive power and sheer physical presence of City's defence in those days. Apart from Leivers himself, the Blues also had Roy Paul and the aforementioned Dave Ewing, none of whom was ever known to shirk a tackle or fail to let the opposition know just what was in store for them. They were so tough at the back that even the goalkeeper played with a broken neck in one game! Leivers was such a determined tackler, often going in where others feared to tread, that during his time at Maine Road he suffered no less than five broken noses, a broken elbow and a broken ankle. A further cartilage operation restricted his appearances to just 12 in 1960-61.

Even though his contemporaries joked he would never win any medals for sprinting, to a man, they all confirmed just what a good reader of the game he was, a talent that more than made up for any shortcomings in the speed department. With the man playing directly in front of him, Ken Barnes, forever going AWOL because of the Revie Plan, Leivers was also expected to cover his position as well.

An ever-present in the 1956-57 campaign, Leivers only representative honour came in November that season when he represented the FA in a game against the Army. With Birmingham's Jeff Hall and later Don Howe of Arsenal tying up England's right-back spot for the bulk of Leivers' playing career, he was unfortunate to be in such good company. As for the centre-half berth, it seemed as though Billy Wright of Wolves had been there forever and would continue to be so.

After 98 games for the reserves and exactly 250 League games for the first team, Leivers was transferred to Doncaster Rovers for a fee of £1,000 on 10 July 1964 to become their player-manager. He did such a good job at Doncaster that they were crowned champions of the Fourth Division two years later. However they did it without Leivers (or anyone else for that matter) in charge. He'd had a dispute with the board and left the club three months before the end of the season. It seemed he'd taken his no-nonsense style from the field into the manager's office.

He was later manager at Workington Town, Cambridge United, Chelmsford City and finally Cambridge City before finally retiring as a 57-year-old in 1989. His seven years in charge of Cambridge United were undoubtedly the most successful of his managerial career. During his time with the non-Leaguers they won successive Southern League championships, gained entrance to the Football League and then promotion to the Third Division.

An active member of the Former Players' Association, Bill Leivers was last seen at Maine Road in the winter of 2001 when he made the half-time draw during a First Division game. He received a hearty round of applause from a good percentage of the 33,000 plus crowd, those of a certain age remembering just what a fine servant he'd been. The applause was thoroughly deserved.

....

Maine Road career

282 appearances   4 goals

Roy Little – stuck like glue

ANOTHER member of the strong City side of the mid-1950s, left-back Roy Little played in successive FA Cup Finals in 1955 and 1956. By coincidence it was in that same competition that he'd made his first appearance in City's colours, a 7-0 demolition of Swindon Town in January 1953.

The following week he marched out proudly at Anfield for his debut in League football, yet again, thanks to Johnny Hart's solitary goal (the same player had scored four against Swindon), Little was on the winning side. There seemed nothing to this top-flight football, although the player had waited a long while to be given a chance at it.

Little had originally signed for the Blues on 6 August 1949 from amateur side Greenwood Victoria. It was the beginning of a nine-year career at Maine Road. After earning his spurs in the reserve side (he would eventually play 87 times in the Central League) Little's chance in the first team finally came when the long-serving Eric Westwood retired midway through that 1952-53 season. Initially it was to be a short courtship with the first team. Little played three games in both the League and the FA Cup before returning to the reserves as Jack Hannaway took over for the remaining three months.

After just two League games of the following season he was back in the first team and would become the first-choice left-back for the next six. The 1953-54 season was a particularly good one for the Manchester-born Little. Not only did he finally establish himself in the side but he also scored his only two goals in what would eventually be a career taking in the best part of 200 games. Those strikes came in a 1-1 draw at Huddersfield and a 3-2 win against Middlesbrough at Maine Road.

Not for the first or last time, City were showing their likeness for the unpredictable, a likeness that meant the early 1950s were years of uncertainty and struggle. Little was given a chance to shine in these lean years and was praised in contemporary newspaper reports for his tough tackling and general overall play. With the introduction of the Revie Plan at the start of the 1954-55 season, City's fortunes were to change dramatically.

Little was a vital if overlooked member of the side that played in this revolutionary new way, a way that would send them to Wembley for back-to-back Finals. In those two seasons he missed just four League games and they were all in the one campaign; he was ever present in 1955-56. Fans and the media tend to voice the majority of their support and praise on the creative players and goalscorers, a perfectly understandable situation. And yet players such as Roy Little, and for that matter his opposite full-back Bill Leivers, are equally as important to a side if not quite as 'glamourous'. Little turned in many sterling performances for the Blues, constantly harrying and frustrating the opposition with his dogged determination. It is only when a side has a mixture of Littles and Revies will it ever prove to be a successful one. A team full of either will always find things difficult.

Bert Trautmann once said of Little, "he liked to get his fangs into an opponent", and he played this way every time he pulled on the sky-blue shirt. It seemed to be the perfect description of this most tenacious defender. Not only could he tackle and distribute the ball well from the back but he also had the reputation of being a very funny man, one who could inject humour into the most serious of dressing rooms. In his early days with City's first team he probably had ample opportunities to practice his comedic talents.

On 18 October 1958, still only 27, he was transferred to newly-promoted Second Division Brighton for a fee of £4,850; his place at Maine Road was taken by the future Welsh international Cliff Sear. After three years on the south coast Little joined Crystal Palace before finishing his playing days with Southern League Dover Athletic as player-manager in 1963.

Despite his years down south Little still loved the city of his birth and returned to Manchester to begin work in the motor auction business. He later worked at the Manchester University sports complex in Wythenshawe. Today Roy Little shows he's not lost any of his old tenacity as he carries out his duties for the club's Former Players Association.

Maine Road career

187 appearances   2 goals

Billy McAdams – goal, goal, goal

FOR seven years during the 1950s the name Billy McAdams was well known at Maine Road. It is somewhat surprising therefore that it should be to some extent forgotten amidst the more famous ones such as Trautmann, Paul and Revie.

One word sums up McAdams; goalscorer. During his time with City he averaged a goal every other game and scored in an amazing run of 10 consecutive matches between 9 October and 7 December 1957. Unquestionably many have scored more times than McAdams but 10 consecutive scoring games is an achievement held exclusively by McAdams as far as City's records go. For good measure he scored twice in the 6-2 defeat of Everton in the tenth game to take his fully tally to 11 in 10. In that same game, Ken Barnes scored a hat-trick of penalties.

After trials with Burnley and Oldham Athletic, the Belfast-born centre-forward joined City from Distillery in December 1953 and made his debut on 2 January, scoring the equaliser against Sunderland at a fog-bound Maine Road. His next game, seven days later, was at Bradford in the FA Cup third round. The Blues won 5-2 with McAdams netting a hat-trick. Obviously liking scoring for the Blues, he continued the following Saturday when he levelled the scores in front of 46,000 at Old Trafford. Five goals in his first three games made Les McDowall's £10,000 investment seem extremely worthwhile and not surprisingly McAdams became very popular with the fans very quickly.

For all his prowess in front of goal, McAdams could also 'play a bit'. Regretably though, a series of injuries (including ankle and head) prevented him from playing as many games as he, and the fans would have liked. His most serious injury was sustained in a friendly at Millwall in October 1954. Chasing a long ball, he failed to stop in time and collided with the surrounding wall, back first. He tried manfully to continue the season but six weeks later he was in hospital having a major operation. The operation and recovery time meant he missed the entire 1955-56 season, as well as the opportunity to play in successive FA Cup Finals. Even worse for the Northern Ireland international was the fact he wasn't allowed on the open-top bus after City's triumph over Birmingham. This after the club had 'generously' paid for him to travel to London on a third class rail ticket.

By the time the 1958 World Cup Finals came around, McAdams was back in City's first team and selected by his country for the tournament in Sweden. He was to receive another setback when his employers told him that he would have to miss the World Cup because City needed his services on their tour of North America and Canada. In later years McAdams perhaps understandably thinks he was undervalued at Maine Road, although also claims his unfortunate injury record probably didn't help matters.

His best season for City was 1959-60 when he played 31 League games (the most he'd ever played in one season), scored 21 times (the most he'd ever scored in one season) and finished top scorer. Despite the appearance of getting over all his injury worries, McAdams found himself being sold to Bolton Wanderers for £25,000 in September the following year. The arrival of British record signing Denis Law in the March may have had something to do with his transfer.

After Bolton he played a short while at Leeds before helping Brentford gain promotion from the Fourth Division. In 1964 he joined Queen's Park Rangers, finishing his career at Barrow three years later where he again won promotion from the Fourth Division.

Today the 68-year-old McAdams still lives within earshot of Barrow's ground, surrounded by his footballing memories, plays golf and pays an occasional visit to Maine Road.

Maine Road career

134 appearances   65 goals

Mick McCarthy – bark and bite

WHEN Republic of Ireland's captain Roy Keane returned home from the World Cup finals in the summer of 2002 (before a ball had even been kicked) it confirmed the old adage 'a leopard can't change its spots'. Ireland's manager Mick McCarthy has never been a man to back down easily. City fans who saw him in action at the centre of the Blues' defence in the mid-1980s already knew that. All Keane had to do was ask them, to realise he was on a loser in any kind of confrontation with the straight-talking manager. The unpleasantness could easily have been avoided, but McCarthy was proved right in the end as his Irish side battled through the group stage manfully only to lose to Spain in the cruelest way of all, on penalties. All this without their influential skipper as well.

Still one of the game's most honest professionals, McCarthy was born in Barnsley in February 1959. After playing for Worsbrough Bridge Athletic in his teens, he joined his hometown club as an apprentice in the summer of 1977 and quickly established himself as the first-choice centre-half. At 6ft 2ins height and weighing a little over 12st he possessed all the necessary physical attributes to make him one of the most respected and feared defenders in the lower divisions and twice won promotion with the Oakwell side.

A virtual ever-present for Barnsley for six seasons, he'd scored ten times in 315 games by the time Billy McNeill secured his services for the Blues by way of a £200,000 transfer fee on 14 December 1989. Many City fans were already well aware of McCarthy, who'd played against them in an inglorious League Cup defeat two years previously.

As a replacement for Tommy Caton who'd moved to Highbury, McCarthy's debut came three days after his arrival at Maine Road, in a goalless draw (in front of just 5,204) at Cambridge. Within five short months of putting pen to paper he'd been made captain and had won the Player of the Year award. Not for the first (or last) time, City's supporters had showed their affection for a player who regularly played his heart out for the cause.

McCarthy's time at Maine Road proved not to be the most successful in the club's history. Despite a seemingly never-ending battle against dwindling finances off the pitch, as well as more than the occasional disappointment on it, a man who won 22 of his 57 Irish caps whilst with City organised a constantly changing side to such a degree that promotion was won in 1985. On the final day of the season City needed to beat Charlton Athletic at home to finish in third spot and kill off any ambitions Portsmouth (same points but an inferior goal-difference) may have had.

In front of more than 47,000 basking in the Maine Road sunshine, City won 5-1 but McCarthy had to watch the game from the stands as a suspension prevented him from taking part in the action. It didn't prevent him from taking part in the celebrations afterwards, though. Still fully clothed, he was hauled head first into the players' bath by his delighted team-mates.

Like George Heslop before him, McCarthy was not known for his scoring exploits although they both proved a liking for Manchester United. Heslop's header back at Old Trafford in March 1968 set the Blues on course for victory on the night and ultimately the First Division championship. McCarthy's thumping header in front of the North Stand in October 1986 earned the Blues a valuable point as they sat rooted to the bottom of the First Division.

By the end of that 1986-87 season, City had managed to progress by just a single position and were relegated after two seasons back in the top flight. It was McCarthy's last season with the Blues.

On 20 May 1987 he joined Celtic for £400,000. In two years at Parkhead he won two Scottish FA Cups and a Scottish Premiership. After a brief flirtation in French football with Olympique Lyonaise, McCarthy signed for Millwall following a two-month loan period at The Dell. Not only did this prove to be his last playing club, it would also prove to be his first experience of management. After captaining Ireland in the 1990 World Cup in Italy he took over at The Den in March 1992 when Bruce Rioch joined Bolton Wanderers.

It was a difficult job taking over from the legendary Jack Charlton as manager of the Republic of Ireland and yet McCarthy so far has at least equalled (some might say bettered) his achievements. After the disappointment of losing out in a play-off for Euro 2000, he rallied his troops magnificently as the 2002 World Cup approached. There's an expression that goes, "His bark's worse than his bite." In McCarthy's case that's not quite true; he has equal amounts of both. Just ask any centre-forward who came up against him. Oh, and Roy Keane.

Maine Road career

163 appearances   3 goals

Les McDowall – boot room to boardroom

LES McDowall, the son of a Scottish missionary, was born in Gunga Pur, India on 25 October 1912. On their return to England, the McDowall's settled in the North-east where the teenage Les began his career as a draughtsman in a Wearside shipyard. After being made redundant in the early 1930s, the football-mad McDowall set about forming his own team – Glenryan Thistle – one that would be made up entirely of players in the same situation as McDowall. It was during a game for Glenryan that McDowall's talents were spotted by Sunderland who offered him a contract on Christmas Eve 1932.

Although undoubtedly grateful for the employment, by 14 March 1938 he'd only played 13 times for Sunderland and accepted a move to Maine Road. McDowall's fee was £7,000, surprisingly high for one who'd played so little professional football, but Wilf Wild saw him as more than a reserve player.

McDowall's arrival towards the end of the 1937-38 season (the one immediately after City had won the First Division title) could not prevent them from slipping into the Second Division. The versatile half-back replaced another former Sunderland player, Bobby Marshall, and was made captain of the Blues until the outbreak of war, during which he returned to draughtsmanship, this time at a local aircraft factory, an occupation that gave him enough free time to be able to turn out for the Blues in more than 100 wartime games.

He was nearly 34 by the time normal football resumed in August 1946 when he handed the captaincy over to Sam Barkas. McDowall played 35 times that season as the Blues won the Second Division title. He played the bulk of the 1947-48 season in the reserves, captaining the side. In November 1949 he became player-manager at Wrexham, a job that kept him away from Maine Road for just eight months.

Once again the Blues had been relegated and on his return as manager in the summer of 1950 (after the departure of Jock Thomson) his brief was a short one; promotion. McDowall immediately signed the inspirational Roy Paul and promotion was achieved at the first time of asking.

And so started a managerial reign that would last for 13 years, a reign that still makes McDowall the club's longest serving post-war manager. In these days of instant success, it seems as though his record will remain intact for a good few years yet. Only Wilf Wild (who managed the club throughout World War Two) has been in charge longer.

McDowall was a great thinker about the game, a man constantly on the look out for new styles of play. One of these was of course the famous deep-lying centre-forward method, one that became known as the Revie Plan and which carried the Blues to successive Cup Finals in the mid-1950s. Another one was the short-lived Marsden Plan, this time involving inside-left Keith Marsden playing alongside Dave Ewing as twin centre-halves. After crushing 6-1 and 9-2 defeats (in the space of a week, at Preston and West Bromwich), it was abandoned.

During his time as manager McDowall bought in the goalscoring talents of Peter Dobing and George Hannah – not to mention Denis Law, albeit for one season – and Bobby Kennedy arrived from Kilmarnock in an attempt to strengthen the defence. However his final years at the helm produced periods of inconsistency and disappointment. Fans and players alike began to question his constant 'tinkering' with the side and it seemed like no one was quite sure just what system was being played at any given time. For instance in 1960-61 the Blues conceded six at West Bromwich and at Chelsea and five at Aston Villa, Arsenal and, worst of all for City fans, Manchester United. In between times, Cardiff, Blackburn and Aston Villa (in the return game) all had four put past them. This was also the season Denis Law scored six in an abandoned FA Cup tie at Luton and still finished on the losing side.

In May 1963, needing a win in their last game to have any chance of avoiding relegation, City travelled to West Ham and lost 6-1. That cost McDowall his job, although it was the Blues' first relegation since McDowall himself had won promotion 12 years earlier. He later became manager of Oldham, his last job in football. He died in August 1991, shortly before his 79th birthday.

Maine Road career

126 appearances   8 goals   (not including wartime appearances)

Jimmy McMullan – a real Scottish wizard

QUITE remarkably, Aston Villa, one of the oldest clubs in the country, failed to appoint their first manager proper until May 1934. Since turning professional some 49 years earlier, just two men – George Ramsay and W.J. Smith – had combined the duties of team matters along with those of the secretary. The honour of being Villa's first-ever manager fell to a 5ft 5ins tall Scotsman called Jimmy McMullan.

At the time of his appointment at Villa Park, McMullan had just turned 39 and already had managerial experience with Oldham Athletic.

He'd also had a non-too inconsiderable playing career as well. Born in the Stirlingshire town of Denny on 26 March 1895, McMullan began his playing days with the town's famous Hibs side, later joined Third Lanark and finally Partick Thistle as an 18-year-old in November 1913. He collected a Scottish Cup winners' medal with Partick in 1921, the culmination of many fine performances that prompted a £5,000 transfer bid from Newcastle United. The Scottish club declined the offer but so determined was McMullan to play in England that he walked out on the Firhill side and became player-manager with non-League Maidstone United.

In the summer of 1923 McMullan was back with Partick, no doubt much wiser in the ways of running a small club. It was a grounding that would serve him well in later years. His two years with Maidstone were by no means the end of his days south of the border.

On 10 February 1926, Partick accepted City's bid of £4,700 and the 30-year-old McMullan, a full Scottish international, moved to Manchester. An intelligent half-back who was an excellent passer of the ball, McMullan was described by one contemporary journalist as "a superb tactician". After making his debut in a 1-1 draw with Liverpool on 27 February, McMullan would display all these qualities in City's colours for the next eight seasons.

Regretably they would come to nothing in his debut season as City (with McMullan in the side and reported to be the game's outstanding player) lost the FA Cup Final to Bolton and were relegated the very next week.

At the start of the 1926-27 season McMullan was promoted to captain. It was an attempt by manager Peter Hodge to use all his canny know-how to win promotion at the earliest possible opportunity. It so very nearly worked. Despite the Blues winning the last game of the season 8-0 at home to Bradford City, they lost out on second place to Portsmouth by the narrowest margin ever. Even though they'd scored 21 more goals than Portsmouth (108 to 87), City's goal difference was 1.7705 against Portsmouth's 1.7755. To get so close and still miss out was arguably worse than the Cup Final defeat and relegation of 12 months earlier. The following year, 1928, was a particularly pleasing one for McMullan. In City's colours he scored four times (his best ever return), captained the Blues to the title that had eluded them so closely the year before and skippered his country to an amazing 5-1 win at Wembley. The papers christened McMullan's victorious Scots the Wembley Wizards in the days immediately after the game.

In 1933 he was back again at Wembley, this time, unfortunately again in City's colours, he was on the losing side against Dixie Dean's Everton. So upset was McMullan at losing his second FA Cup Final that he broke down in tears at the final whistle. Just over a fortnight later the 38-year-old left Maine Road and joined Oldham Athletic as player-manager, thereby missing the Blues' success against Portsmouth (the team had beaten them by the smallest of goal average differences) at Wembley in 1934.

McMullan's solitary season in charge at Oldham saw the Latics finish ninth in Division Two (11 places above Manchester United) and reach the Lancashire Senior Cup Final. Between May 1934 and October 1936 he was the inaugural manager at Villa Park before a 12-month stint with Notts. County. His final club was Sheffield Wednesday, one who provided him with his longest time in the manager's chair. After joining just before Christmas 1937 he saved them from relegation to the Third Division and then missed out on promotion back to Division One (ironically to Sheffield rivals United) by a single point in 1939. When his contract at Hillsborough expired in 1942 it was not renewed. He continued to live in Sheffield and died there on 28 November 1964, aged 69.

Jimmy McMullan Walk, just off Claremont Road close to the ground in Moss Side, stands as a permanent reminder to a most gifted footballer, one who won eight of his 16 Scottish caps whilst on City's books.

Maine Road career

242 appearances   12 goals

Neil McNab – tremendous value for money

A COMMITTED and tough-tackling midfielder, Neil McNab was Billy McNeill's first signing for City when he took over the manager's reigns at Maine Road in the summer of 1983. Having been relegated at the end of the previous season (in the last game against David Pleat's Luton) McNeill paid Brighton £35,000 for McNab's fighting qualities, qualities that would certainly be needed if promotion was to be assured.

A native of Greenock just outside Glasgow, McNab's career started with his local club Morton in 1973. He was only 16 when he moved south to Tottenham the following February, the fee of £40,000 thought large at the time for someone with such limited experience. He stayed at White Hart Lane for four years, winning promotion with them in 1977-78, by which time he had been capped at Under-21 level and established himself in the first team. The arrival of Argentinean World Cup winners Osvaldo Ardiles and Ricky Villa in September 1978 put an end to his time with Tottenham where he'd played in more than seventy League games.

He joined Bolton where his tenacity endeared him to the supporters quickly. Despite his best efforts he was playing in a poor Bolton side and by the time they were relegated two years later he'd already packed his bags and moved to Brighton. Although he played over 100 times in the League for the south coast side he could not seem to be classed as a permanent fixture in the team and consequently had loan spells with both Leeds and Portsmouth. When he signed for City, any uncertainties about his place in the starting line-up were long gone.

His debut came on the opening day of the 1983-84 season in a 2-0 Maine Road victory over Crystal Palace. He played 33 times that season, scoring once, however his strike at Craven Cottage in March hardly affected the outcome of the game as Fulham scored five at the other end. City finished the season in fourth place, a 5-0 win against Cambridge in the last game giving fans some encouragement for the next time of asking.

In only the fourth game of what turned out to be a promotion campaign, McNab was injured against Wolves. It was the first of three injuries that limited his appearances to 17 starts in all competitions that season although he was back in the side by the time promotion was clinched with a 5-1 win against Charlton.

The mid-to-late 1980s were (once again) topsy turvey times at Maine Road. Relegation, promotion and an appearance in the Full Members' Cup Final at Wembley all came and went during that time. Perhaps the only consistent factor in those four years was Neil McNab; he seemed to be always in the thick of the action, sleeves proverbially rolled up, battling away for the City cause. An ever-present in both 1986-87 and 1988-89, McNab was voted the club's Player of the Year for the same two seasons.

On 7 November 1987, City crushed Huddersfield 10-1 at Maine Road to record the club's biggest win of the century. With Paul Stewart, Tony Adcock and David White each scoring hat-tricks, the honour of scoring the other fell to Neil McNab. Almost 15 years on, his opener still provides the occasional quiz question.

By January 1990 new manager Howard Kendall had begun to make changes to the team, not least in McNab's midfield area. McNab (with another crowd favourite Ian Bishop) found himself being replaced by a combination of new arrivals Gary Megson, Mark Ward and Peter Reid and a transfer seemed imminent.

And so it proved. He joined Third Division Tranmere Rovers for £125,000, a more than satisfactory return on the outlay of seven years earlier. At Prenton Park he helped Tranmere gain promotion via the play-offs, appeared at Wembley in two Leyland Daf Finals and played 105 League games in a little over two years. After Tranmere he became somewhat of a Romany, stopping off at Huddersfield, Ayr, Darlington, Derry City and finally Witton Albion before hanging up his boots and returning to Maine Road as Youth Team coach in 1994.

McNab's first arrival at Maine Road coincided with a shortage of cash following the big-spending period of some four years earlier. Had money been available, it seems perfectly plausible to assume that the club would have blown it on one big-name midfielder. Thankfully they didn't.

Maine Road career

261-5 appearances   19 goals

Ernest Mangnall – look to the future

LIKE countless men in the history of football, Ernest Mangnall loved the game so much as a youngster that he hoped one day to fulfil his ambitions as a player. And yet, like the vast majority of those concerned, his ability failed to live up to his dreams and he had to settle for playing local amateur football in his native Bolton and surrounding Lancashire. Whilst no mean goalkeeper himself he was also more than a capable rugby player, cycling road racer and a cross country runner with Bolton Harriers.

Mangnall realised that if he could not contribute on the pitch then he would harness all his energies into the administrative side of a game blossoming at the turn of the last century. In January 1900 he became secretary-manager at Burnley having already spent a short while as a director of Bolton Wanderers. It was at Burnley that he really learned the 'tricks of the trade' that would stand him in good stead in later years. Although Burnley were a struggling side (in fact they finished bottom of the Second Division in 1903) Mangnall displayed both fine administrative skills, and perhaps even more important, the capability to work on the proverbial shoestring budget. It was these qualities that led to an offer from Manchester United just a few short weeks after finishing in that bottom spot.

Mangnall stayed with United for nine years and took them from an average Second Division side to First Division champions and FA Cup winners and was a key figure in their move from Clayton to Old Trafford. Helped by the arrival of some of City's banned players (including Billy Meredith and Sandy Turnbull) it was undoubtedly Mangnall who turned United into one of the country's biggest clubs.

Not least in the North-West, everyone connected with game was shocked when, in September 1912, he left the successes of United to move across town to Hyde Road. Possibly Mangnall had felt he'd achieved all he could with the Reds and wanted to try and repeat the formula with the Blues who at the time were marginally the poorer neighbours, but certainly the less successful. Ironically Mangnall's last game in charge of United was against his new club on 12 September 1912. Thanks to a solitary goal by City's George Wynn, the Blues won at Old Trafford for the first time ever in a game set aside as Billy Meredith's testimonial. The Welshman would be £2,000 better off at the end of it as his former manager looked forward to the challenges ahead.

Regretably though Mangnall was unable to reproduce his magic at Hyde Road. Having said that however there were some significant highlights during his 12 years with City. Having shown a rise of nine places in Division One in his first season, the Blues then finished runners-up in 1921. In 1923 the club moved to their brand new Maine Road stadium with the ambitious Mangnall, as he was at United 13 years before, a key figure in their development. For almost half his time with City Mangnall had to deal with the effects of World War One and all its restrictions. Although he was unquestionably more successful with United, Mangnall should be praised for keeping the club afloat during these difficult times, the Hyde Road ground being used for stables just one of the many hardships suffered.

In May 1924, just five weeks after being beaten in the FA Cup semi-final by Newcastle, Mangnall's contract was not renewed by the club and he returned to his former position on the board at Bolton. At the time it was felt by many to be a strange decision, after all it was City who were now a division higher than their neighbours and currently showed a bank balance of more than £25,000. When Mangnall originally took charge it had been less than £100.

As well as furthering the development of Manchester football, Mangnall was also a founder member of the Central League and the Football Managers' Association. For his services to the game he was awarded a long-service medal in 1921 and the proceeds from a combined Manchester and Liverpool game three years later.

A key figure in establishing the game during its formative years, Ernest Mangnall, the only man to manage both Manchester clubs, died in 1932.

Rodney Marsh – a great entertainer

BY his own admittance, Rodney Marsh cost City the First Division championship in 1972. Marsh's confessions came in his autobiography published almost 30 years after the event and yet harsh statistics may offer a different opinion. Fans too have mixed recollections and opinions; the numbers agreeing with the player equalling those who don't.

After a search going on for the best part of two years Malcolm Allison had finally raised sufficient funds to buy Marsh in March 1972 from Queen's Park Rangers. He'd had to sell both Neil Young and David Connor to Preston to come up with the final installment of the £200,000 fee, an amount that more than tripled the existing club transfer record of £65,000 for Arthur Mann. Marsh's debut came against Chelsea on 18 March in front of a crowd of 53,322, more than 9,000 up on the previous home gate two weeks earlier against Arsenal. Thanks to a solitary goal from Tommy Booth City won the game 1-0 but it was an eye-opener for Marsh. The player was both overweight and unfit for First Division football, and, as well as suffering from nervous tension, was replaced by Tony Towers shortly before the end of the game.

He played a part in all bar one of the remaining eight games (scoring four times), a sequence in which the Blues lost twice. There was no doubting his obvious ability. Anyone who saw him standing on the ball and telling United's defenders to come and try and take it off him or his goal against Derby County in the final game of the season still remember those incidents today. These were perfect examples of the kind of showmanship and skill Malcolm Allison knew he was capable of. What was in doubt though was his particular style of play and whether it would fit in at Maine Road or disrupt what had proved to be the successful formula of the past few years. With Summerbee, Bell and Lee rampaging forward waiting for a through ball, the flamboyant Marsh would be stood on it in the centre-circle trying to nutmeg a bamboozled defender. With hindsight it probably wasn't exactly the right thing to do and perhaps it did prove costly in the end. It was great entertainment nonetheless. As time went on though the City fans went home unhappy when he hadn't turned in one of his solo performances. The Hatfield-born Marsh became hugely popular on the terraces, the sheer volume of noise indicating that if indeed he had cost the Blues the title, he'd most certainly been forgiven for it. He became idolised at Maine Road in the same way he'd been at Loftus Road.

As a youngster Marsh had collided with a goalpost and suffered partial deafness, an injury that at first put his football aspirations on hold. However this most skilful of players wasn't going let anything stand in his way and by the time he was 18 he'd signed apprentice forms for Fulham. At Craven Cottage he would eventually graduate to the first team playing many of his 63 League games for Fulham alongside his boyhood hero Johnny Haynes. In 1966 he was transferred to Queen's Park Rangers where he developed so much that even playing for a then Third Division side his reputation spread throughout the country. Playing for QPR against West Bromwich Albion in the 1967 League Cup Final Marsh scored a brilliant solo goal, one that swung the game and eventually caused a surprise result. With successive promotions and his first England cap behind him, Rangers' fans were as determined to keep him as Allison was to get him, but, back in the days of flares and bushy sideburns, £200,000 was an awful lot for a footballer and so Marsh became a City player.

For almost four seasons he was arguably the biggest star in a star-studded City team that even included the returning Denis Law for a while. With such an array of talent available it is perhaps surprising that his only domestic honour with the Blues was a League Cup runners'-up medal in 1974. He won his remaining eight England caps whilst with City, a figure reasonably high when you think of the way Marsh played and the fact that the conservative Alf Ramsey was in charge of the national side at the time.

In January 1976 he left City and moved to Tampa Bay Rowdies of the NASL, a country and newly developing League that seemed to fit Marsh perfectly. As time went on he became the driving force behind a team that would rival the New York Cosmos as the best and most glamourous team in the country. A break from the Florida sunshine saw him return to his first club Fulham where he played 16 times with his great friends George Best and Bobby Moore. Not surprisingly with these three legends of British football playing in the same side, tickets for home games at Craven Cottage were at a premium.

In more recent times Marsh has become a television pundit with Sky TV and is a man known for pulling no punches with his opinions. As a more than welcome visitor to City's Supporters' Club meetings, it seems he's lost none of his popularity with the Maine Road faithful.

Maine Road career
150-2 appearances   47 goals

Bobby Marshall – a fine conversion job

BORN in the Nottinghamshire town of Hucknall on 3 April 1903, Bobby Marshall was a skilful, ball-playing inside-forward who joined Sunderland in 1920 from his home-town side Olympia.

He stayed at Roker Park for the best part of eight years, arriving at Maine Road somewhat surprisingly on a free transfer on 1 March 1928. Whilst in the north-east Marshall scored 71 times in over 200 games, his most prolific period being April 1927 when he scored back-to-back hat-tricks against Arsenal and Bolton Wanderers.

Blues' manager Peter Hodge was hoping Marshall would be just the player his team needed on the last lap of their push for the Second Division title. And so it proved. Marshall played in the last 14 games of the season (his debut coming in a 4-1 win against Blackpool), a run that contained just two defeats and culminated in the championship with a two-point gap from Leeds United. The player's personal contribution to that success was seven goals, including a hat-trick against Southampton (City winning 6-1) in the penultimate game.

For the next 10 years Marshall was a key figure in the fortunes of Manchester City. In each of the first two of those seasons – 1928-29 and 1929-30 – the free-flowing City attackers scored more than 90 goals in the League and 19 times in six FA Cup ties. In a 4th round replay against Swindon Town in January 1930, Marshall scored five of City's 10. The game finished 10-1 and still stands as the club's record Cup victory. Not counting Denis Law's abandoned six against Luton, Marshall is one of only five players who ever achieved this remarkable feat for City. Only one player has managed it since; George Smith in 1947. Marshall's 21 goals in all competitions in that year made it his best ever for City.

Although Marshall had proved he was more than a capable goalscorer, the Blues still had players of the calibre of Eric Brook, Fred Tilson and David Halliday in their attack and as a result Marshall eventually adapted to a role just behind this front three. It was a leg injury to Tilson that gave Roberts the opportunity to play up front in the 1933 FA Cup Final against Everton. Nervous on the day, City did themselves no justice and lost 3-0.

As captain Sam Cowan had promised, the Blues were back the following year and against Portsmouth showed their true ability. Tilson had managed to shake of his earlier injury and thanks to his goals, City came back from a goal down to win 2-1. Just three weeks after celebrating his 31st birthday, Bobby Marshall was two places behind his captain anxiously waiting to collect his winners' medal from King George V. In that very same year, Marshall also received a benefit cheque of £650 for his services to City. All in all, 1934 was a very good year for this most likeable of players.

When Peter Doherty arrived in February 1936, Wilf Wild asked Marshall to revert to centre-half in order to accommodate the brilliant Irishman. Always a team player, Marshall took to his new role as easily as if he'd been born to it. He seemed as much at home stopping goals as he had all those years scoring and providing them, mind you, perhaps he more than most, knew just what the attackers were thinking. Centre-half was to be his regular position for his next three (and final years) with the club. It was almost like a new, second career for Marshall.

In 1936-37, he played in more League games (38 of a possible 42) than in any of his previous seasons. Starting with a 2-1 Boxing Day win against Middlesbrough, City embarked on an unbeaten run (14 runs and 6 draws) through to the end of that season, one that saw them win the First Division championship for the first time. Marshall missed just one of those last 20 games, and whilst undoubtedly Doherty's goals were a crucial part of the success, Marshall's organising and tightening of the defence should not go unnoticed.

That championship season was to be Marshall's penultimate one with City. On 22 March 22 1939 he became manager at Third Division North Stockport County, a position he'd hold throughout the war before moving to Chesterfield in February 1949. Under Marshall the Derbyshire side finished sixth in Division Two that year, above more illustrious names such as West Ham, Leeds United and Nottingham Forest.

Perhaps a name not too familiar to City fans, Bobby Marshall should be remembered as a man who contributed a huge amount to one of the most successful period's in the club's history. For instance he scored more goals for the Blues than Mike Summerbee and Roy Clarke and most people know what great players they were.

Maine Road career

356 appearances   80 goals

Joe Mercer OBE – a true ambassador for the game

QUITE simply as a player, manager and later ambassador, this quietly spoken man from the Wirral was without doubt one of the greatest figures ever to appear in the professional game in England. Born in Ellesmere Port on 9 August 1914, Joe Mercer's father (Joe senior) had been a regular centre-half for Tranmere Rovers and Nottingham Forest until the outbreak of World War One stripped him of his best playing years. By the time he was 15, Joe junior had signed schoolboy forms for Everton, the club he supported as a youngster.

When World War Two arrived in September 1939, Mercer (at left-half) was a vital cog in the Everton wheel that had clinched the First Division championship just a few months earlier. He had also won five England caps, a figure that would rise to 31 by the end of hostilities six years later.

In December 1946, aged 32, Mercer joined Arsenal with many people saying that he'd gone down to London purely to play for a couple of seasons and to see his career out. Remarkably nearly eight years later he was still playing. Had it not been for suffering a broken leg in a bizarre collision with his Arsenal teammate Joe Wade, it was thought he could still have continued.

The 40-year-old Mercer had no option but to go back to the Wirral and the family grocery business. It was scant consolation for a man who lived and breathed football. In the summer of 1956 he had the opportunity to return to the game when he took over the vacant managerial position at Sheffield United. Looking back this was no doubt good experience for the years ahead but the disappointing crowd reaction and a desperate shortage of finance meant it was undoubtedly a difficult time for him. By the time Christmas 1958 had arrived, Mercer found himself behind a new desk; this time at Villa Park. He brought promotion, a League Cup triumph (Villa were its first winners) and two FA Cup semi-finals in six years. And yet Villa (and once again Joe Mercer) found themselves with financial worries. Just a few weeks short of his 50th birthday, Mercer suffered a stroke.

Doctors ordered complete rest away from the game and for 12 months Mercer – much to his wife Norah's obvious pleasure – stuck rigidly to their instructions. However his life (and that of Manchester City) was to change dramatically on 13 July 1965 when City chairman Albert Alexander telephoned him and asked him to take over at his ailing football club. Despite the obvious medical concerns it was too good an opportunity for a man still in love with the game to turn down. Realising his limitations with regard to the training pitch activities, Mercer insisted in bringing in a younger, fitter man to take over that side of things for him. The man he chose was the former West Ham defender but now somewhat controversial and outspoken coach Malcolm Allison. It was a match made in heaven.

Over the next seven years these two men made Manchester City into one of the best sides not only in the country, but also in Europe. By the end of their first season together they'd won the Second Division championship. Two years later they'd brought the First Division championship trophy to Moss Side for the first time in more than 30 years, with the FA Cup following in 1969. The victory over Leicester City meant Mercer had become the first man to win the FA Cup as both a player and a manager.

The next year continued in the same vein and when City beat Polish side Gornik Zabrze to win the European Cup-winners' Cup to go alongside the League Cup they'd already taken from the hands of West Bromwich Albion, it meant City were the first team to win both a domestic and European trophy in the same season. Heady days indeed for supporters of Manchester City.

As with all good things though, it had to end some time or another. In 1971 Allison was given responsibility solely for team affairs with Mercer being promoted 'upstairs' and given the title of general manager. It was a situation that in the end suited and benefited absolutely no one (least of all the club) and by June 1972 Mercer had taken up a similar position with Coventry City. In 1974, following the dismissal of Sir Alf Ramsey, Mercer took over the national side for a hugely enjoyable seven-match period. It was the last managerial job he held in football although he did stay on as a director of Coventry until 1981.

His final years were spent on the Wirral with his beloved Norah but he kept in touch with the game by being a regular visitor to Tranmere Rovers as well as being one of the most popular after-dinner speakers on the circuit.

As he entered his 70s, he tragically became the victim of Alzheimer's Disease and on 9 August 1990, his 76th birthday, Joe Mercer passed away peacefully at home in his favourite armchair. Football had lost one of its most popular figures; a man loved by everyone in the game, especially those connected with Manchester City.

Billy Meredith – the Welsh Wizard

IN 1894, a skinny, bandy-legged 20-year-old miner thought nothing of travelling 60 miles in any direction to play a game of football. His name was Billy Meredith and whatever transport he could muster would take him regularly from his hometown of Chirk in Denbighshire to Northwich Victoria in neighbouring Cheshire. In October that year City secretary (later manager) Lawrence Furniss refereed a match in which Meredith played at Northwich, and his performance convinced Furniss that he must acquire his services for the fledgling Hyde Road club. At first Meredith refused to sign as a professional, saying he didn't want paying to play the game he loved so much. In the end Meredith agreed to sign on as an amateur (for a reported £5 signing on fee) and three months later, in January 1895, he did finally turn professional. It was undoubtedly the best £5 the club has ever spent.

His career at Maine Road was in two clearly defined parts. The first began on 27 October 1894 when (still as an amateur) he made his debut at Newcastle in a game City lost 5-4. Over the next 11 seasons, Meredith became the most admired footballer in the country with only Derby's England centre-forward Steve Bloomer coming anywhere near his popularity. His skill and pace on the wing coupled with his ability to find his teammates with unerring accuracy caused countless problems for opposition defenders as well as many goalscoring opportunities for his colleagues. He was also more than capable of finding the net himself, his goal against Bolton Wanderers in the 1904 FA Cup Final (City winning 1-0) proving the point.

In 1905, as the Blues pressed for the First Division championship, Meredith, along with several other City players, was banned by the FA for allegedly trying to bribe an Aston Villa player. This forced him to move across town to Manchester United where he played nearly 300 games until July 1921. It was at this point (following a dispute about wages at Old Trafford) he returned to Hyde Road as player-coach to begin the second part of his City career. Amazingly he was now five days short of his 47th birthday. During World War One, although registered as a player with United, Meredith turned out more than 100 times in City's colours.

He played his last game (an FA Cup semi-final at St Andrew's) for City ironically against the same team as he played his first, Newcastle United. The date was 29 March 1924, almost 30 years since his debut. Meredith was 49 years, 245 days old, making him not only the oldest player to ever appear in City's first team, but also the oldest player ever to play in the FA Cup for any side.

During an amazing career, the 'Welsh Wizard' won 48 caps (22 of them whilst with City) and scored 151 goals in 394 appearances for the Blues. To go alongside his 1904 FA Cup winners' medal, he also collected Division Two championship medals in 1899 and 1903 with City, as well as another FA Cup and two First Division honours whilst wearing the red of United. Not only was Meredith a wonderful footballer, he also appeared occasionally in the movie reels of the time, endorsed various footballing products and was a cartoonists' favourite because of the way he went everywhere with a toothpick in the corner of his mouth.

In April 1925 a crowd in excess of 15,000 turned up at Maine Road to watch Meredith (now over 50) play for a City side against a combined Glasgow Rangers and Celtic team in his testimonial game. The game finished 2-2 and the gate receipts of £870 showed the esteem the footballing public held him in.

Perhaps not surprisingly after the heights he'd reached in football, Meredith struggled after his retirement. He kept his involvement with the Players' Union (one he was instrumental in starting up) and for a while ran a cinema as well as a sports shop. He seemed happiest though holding fort and talking football with the regulars when he became landlord of the Stretford Road Hotel.

Billy Meredith, one of the greatest names in British football died at his home in Withington in April 1958 at the grand old age of 83 and was buried in Manchester's Southern Cemetery. In January 2002 a story in the press told of a group of City supporters who'd discovered Meredith's grave was in a state of disrepair and tried to do something about it. With the help of Manchester City, Manchester United and the English and Welsh FAs, restoration work was duly carried out and a fine new headstone now proudly marks the final resting place of a true legend of Manchester City.

Hyde Road-Maine Road career

394 appearances   151 goals   (not including wartime games)

William 'Spud' Murphy – keep on runnin'

BY all accounts, both contemporary and those of more recent historians, Billy Murphy was one of the fastest players ever on the club's books.

Not surprisingly he was given the nickname 'Spud' at a very early age, but perhaps what is surprising – given his name – is that he was not born in Ireland. He was actually born in St Helens on 23 March 1895, a fact reported to the Irish FA by City manager Ernest Mangnall when the FAI enquired about his eligibility in a letter to Hyde Road.

In his younger days he'd been a highly thought of cross-country runner with his local Peasley Cross Harriers Club but was lost to athletics when the outbreak of World War One in 1914 caused the club to be disbanded. Prior to more formal racing, some stories also describe the young Murphy's pace being put to use by the pigeon fanciers of St Helens as they employed him to report the birds' arrival times back to headquarters. There seems to be no questioning Murphy's pace and stamina and when he lost the chance to continue his cross-country running he took up football as an alternative. It appeared to be the logical choice and Murphy was most certainly good at it.

His first club was Alexandra Victoria, the club City signed him from on 2 February 1918. It wasn't until the following September – the first full season back after the war – that the 24-year-old was given his debut in the senior side. Replacing Joe Cartwright on the left-wing, Murphy played in a 4-1 defeat by Bolton at Hyde Road. Seven days later, in the return fixture, his new teammates suffered a 6-2 defeat. Although it wasn't the most auspicious of starts, Murphy had begun a run of 36 consecutive games in the League; the only two he missed being the last two of the season. It was a season in which he scored five times in the League, his first brace coming in an 8-2 home win against Blackburn in November with the remainder coming in three successive games over the New Year period. Scoring though wasn't Murphy's job in the team; that was to supply the ammunition for the hugely prolific Tommy Browell and Horace Barnes. With a combined 45 goals between them, Murphy took to his new role quickly and apparently without too much trouble. It was to be a most attractive and fruitful combination for City for the next five years.

Murphy's pace and directness combined with nimble feet quickly made him a firm favourite with the flat-capped masses at Hyde Road. He was in the side when City beat championship rivals Burnley at Hyde Road in March 1921 in front a crowd believed to be in the region of 50,000. By a long way it was the biggest crowd ever seen in Ardwick and when no more spaces could be found on the stand roof, the crowd began to assemble on the touchlines, no doubt restricting Murphy's wing play although not City's overall performance as they ran out 3-0 winners. Two years later Murphy played in another important game in the club's history; the first one at the new stadium in Moss Side. Taking up his usual position wide out on the left, he looked on as goals from Horace Barnes and Tommy Johnson heralded a new era for the club.

Murphy continued to enjoy the new, wide-open spaces of Maine Road but could only manage nine League games in 1925-26 before a move to Southampton in August. Curiously enough at the end of that season, City were relegated. He returned to his native north-west to finish his playing days with Oldham Athletic in 1929.

Billy Murphy played for City during a time of great changes, from the difficult days at the end of World War One through to, and beyond, the move to Hyde Road but unfortunately had no medals to show for his efforts. The nearest he came was a championship runner-up in 1921. Whilst perhaps not as well known as his more illustrious colleagues such as the aforementioned Browell and Barnes as well as the returning Meredith, Murphy's contribution to City should not go entirely unnoticed.

Hyde Road-Maine Road career

220 appearances   31 goals   (not including wartime games)

Alan Oakes – dependable in every way

WHEN Alan Oakes signed for City as an amateur from Mid-Cheshire Boys on 8 April 1958, little did anyone at the time know he'd become a record breaker at the club.

His 676-4 games for the Blues spread over a magnificent 17-year professional career place him at the top of the Blues' appearances table, more than 70 clear of his nearest rival (and long-term teammate) Joe Corrigan. His haul of six winners' medals is also the highest achieved by any one individual during their time with City.

One of the most dependable defender-midfielders ever in the game for any club, Oakes had the misfortune to wear the same number-six shirt as West Ham's Bobby Moore, the England captain of the era and one of the country's finest footballing ambassadors. It was purely down to Moore's presence that Oakes' failed to achieve the international recognition he thoroughly deserved. Many far less talented and committed players than Alan Oakes have been capped for their country. His only representative honour was a solitary appearance for the Football League (against Scotland) in 1969. It was perhaps the one disappointment in his long and illustrious career, although he has gone down on record as saying that Denis Law's 87th-minute penalty for United at Maine Road in May 1963 (to earn a 1-1 draw and effectively condemn the Blues to Division Two) provided him with his worst footballing moment.

His first senior appearance for the Blues was on 14 November 1959, a 1-1 home draw with Chelsea. His last was as a substitute for Mike Doyle in a 2-0 defeat at Old Trafford on 4 May 1976. In between times Oakes, quite literally, was at the heart (he could possibly be described as *the* heart) of almost every single City side. Playing alongside his cousin Glyn Pardoe, Oakes survived the torrid days of the early 1960s to become one of several home-grown youngsters who blossomed under the guidance of Joe Mercer and Malcolm Allison.

A tireless worker for his team, Oakes possessed a marvellous left foot (as well as some huge shin pads!), one that was more than capable of dispossessing an opponent and then firing a 50 or 60 yard pass wide out to the right for Mike Summerbee to run on to. For three consecutive seasons from 1963-64 he played in 41 of the 42 League games, resulting in a Second Division championship winners' medal in 1966. At the time he was still only 23 and a veteran of 239 first team matches. He'd set a pattern that would continue over the next few, halcyon, years.

In the successful First Division championship campaign of 1967-68, once again he missed just one game. His absence from the 5-1 win against Fulham at Maine Road in March coincided with the Blues topping the table for the first time. The triumph at Newcastle on the final day of the season preceded an FA Cup win in 1969, followed by a glorious double of League and European Cup-winners' Cups the following year.

He could hardly be called a prolific goalscorer although when he did manage to find the net it was invariably from outside the penalty area. His best season was 1969-70 when he scored five times in an astonishing 58 games, arguably his best coming in a European clash with Athletic Bilbao at Maine Road. Oakes was admired greatly by managers with other clubs, not least Liverpool's Bill Shankly and Don Revie from Leeds, both of whom commented on his total professionalism.

Having already given City the lead in the semi-final clash with Middlesbrough, he went on to collect his last medal in 1976 as a member of Tony Book's side that beat Newcastle to lift the League Cup. In July that year the Winsford-born Oakes became player-manager with Chester; after all he'd achieved for them the Blues still had the audacity to request (and receive!) a £15,000 fee. He played 211 League games for Chester and guided them to the lofty heights of fifth in Division Three in 1978 as well as the fifth round of the FA Cup twice in four years. In March 1982 Chester dispensed with his services whilst struggling at the bottom of the same division. Oakes then had a couple of brief spells coaching Port Vale and even turned out for them during a player shortage in 1983 as a 41-year-old. At the time of writing Alan's son Michael, another player with a strong left foot, is currently keeping goal for Wolves.

Both on and off the pitch, Alan Oakes was a true professional in every sense of the word. A tremendous athlete and a player who caused referees the minimum of trouble, it seems as though his name will be forever at the top of the appearances table at Manchester City. As the great Yorkshire bowler Fred Trueman once said, "If anyone does break the record, they'll be bloody knackered!"

Maine Road career
676-4 appearances   34 goals

Glyn Pardoe – a one-club man

BOTH as a player and as a coach, Glyn Pardoe's association with Manchester City lasted more than 30 years. It had begun in July 1961 when the former Mid-Cheshire and England Boy signed apprentice forms for Les McDowall. It ended in May 1992, when as a coach for the youth and reserve sides, he was sacked by Peter Reid, a decision that angered many.

At school the Winsford-born Pardoe had displayed his versatility by playing in a variety of positions, including centre-half, inside-forward and centre-forward. By his own admittance, as long as he was playing, anywhere would do him. When he started out at Maine Road it was as a number-nine and it would be in that position that he made his debut against Birmingham in a 4-1 home defeat on 11 April 1962. At the time he had yet to turn professional, and at just 15 years and 315 days old, it also meant he had become the youngest player to appear in City's first team. To date this is still a record and one that probably will never be broken.

In June 1963 he turned professional and was rewarded with 20 starts, his most to date, in the 1963-64 season. It was during that season that he scored his first senior goals – at Huddersfield and Swansea – in the last two away games in April. When Joe Mercer and Malcolm Allison took over in 1965 Pardoe still found himself playing in different positions, in fact he wore five different shirts during the Second Division championship campaign. As the years went on, he would appear in every position for the Blues except goalkeeper and centre-half.

In the early stages of the 1966-67 season he replaced Bobby Kennedy at left-back; at last it seemed as though he'd found his best position. A good tackler and excellent passer of the ball, he was calmness personified, perhaps the biggest asset of all for a defender. In the next four seasons he missed just 10 League games collecting a First Division champions' medal, winning the FA Cup and playing for England Under-23s along the way. At the pinnacle of his career he was very unlucky not to play for his country at the highest level and only just missed out on selection for the Mexico World Cup party.

In March 1970 came possibly his greatest personal moment when he scored the winning goal in extra-time in the League Cup Final against West Bromwich Albion. The goal could not have come at a better moment; it was his one and only of the season. In December the same year he suffered his greatest personal disappointment. Playing in a 4-1 win at Old Trafford, he had his leg broken following a tackle by George Best. The injuries were so severe that at one point it seemed as though it would need to be amputated, although fortunately for the player, expert help was on hand and the leg was saved. However a bone graft was needed and he was out of action for almost two years.

He made a comeback in November 1972 in the 4-0 win against Derby County (one of six games he played in the 1972-73 season), returning back to almost full fitness in readiness for the start of the next. By that time Willie Donachie had taken his place at left-back, Tony Book had retired so Pardoe settled in on the right as if he'd never been away. He played at right-back in the 1974 League Cup Final against Wolves, a game where unfortunately he could not provide the winner a second time.

It was somewhat ironic that after further surgery (this time on his left knee instead of the shattered right leg) he decided to retire from playing in April 1976 shortly before the Blues embarked on a summer tour of the Far East. Because he'd been so heavily involved in training and physiotherapy during his lengthy lay-offs, not surprisingly Pardoe had got caught up with that side of the game, and by the time of the tour he'd become a member of the backroom staff. Travelling with the party he was drafted in for two games against the South Korean National side, the one on 3 June being the last time he'd line up for the Blues.

For the next 16 years he imparted his not inconsiderable knowledge and wisdom to generations of up and coming young footballers. All that was to abruptly end when Reid made his changes. Not surprisingly after such long and loyal service, the quietly spoken Pardoe was devastated by the news and took a year off before finding work with Barclays Bank at their computer centre in Knutsford. The cousin of another City stalwart Alan Oakes, Pardoe was a key member of the great all-conquering Mercer-Allison sides and as such, will always be fondly remembered by City supporters old enough to recall those halcyon days.

Maine Road career
378-2 appearances   22 goals

Roy Paul – a red dragon of Wales

WITH Tony Book, Roy Paul must surely rank as the finest captain Manchester City has ever had. Although not the quickest of players, he was a man who led by example, a fine reader of the game, a fiercely competitive player and a man who captained the Blues in successive FA Cup Finals in the mid-1950s.

Many of his contemporaries, both players and managers, were full of praise for the Welshman's abilities with more than one club keen to have him amongst their ranks. It is remarkable therefore that as a schoolboy, he failed three times in trial matches to earn a place in the school team. One of the reasons given was he wasn't strong enough. Many opposition centre-forwards of the 1950s would suggest that the teacher concerned needed to re-evaluate his opinion.

One of 12 children, Paul was born in the small mining village of Gelli Pentre in South Wales in April 1920. Perhaps spurred on by his failure to make the school team, he worked hard at his game and was eventually chosen to play for the nearby Ton Pentre Boys Club. He later progressed to Ton Pentre's senior side before joining Second Division Swansea Town in 1938. When war broke out the following year he became a PT instructor with the Royal Marines, serving some of his time in India, but managing also to play more than 80 games for Swansea in the wartime League.

On his return, Paul was tempted, along with some other British players, to try his hand in Bogotá, Colombia when he joined FC Millionaros, the prospects of considerable wealth and a place in the sun proving too good to turn down after the hardships and rationing of Britain.

However things didn't quite work out as planned and his stay in South America was a short-lived one. In July 1950, still a Swansea player, he joined City for £19,500; manager Les McDowall had bought a 'rock', one that would be at the heart of City's defence for seven years. His debut came on 19 August in a 4-2 win at Preston, the opening day of a season that would see him miss just one game and City win promotion to the First Division.

Over the next few years Paul was an inspiration to everyone at Maine Road. Even though his occasional liking for a drink didn't go unnoticed it never once affected his performance. Bert Trautmann described him as 'an amazing man' and Roy Clarke said of him, "He looked after every one of us; he was always there". Paul hated to lose and the defeat against Newcastle in the 1955 FA Cup Final hurt him deeply. He was so determined to reproduce the feat of Sam Cowan in the 1930s ("we'll be back next year and win it") that he threatened every one of his teammates with a whole manner of misfortunes if they let him down again the following year. Fortunately (and very wisely) they didn't, City winning 3-1 against Birmingham. Forty-odd years before it became 'fashionable', Roy Paul looked a very pleased man as he stood on the Wembley turf with both the FA Cup and his young son Robert.

He won 24 of his 33 Welsh caps (making him the most-capped Welshman of all time at Maine Road) during his time with City as well as playing for his country against the Rest of the UK in 1951. After playing nearly 300 times for the Blues (he was by now 37 years old) Paul left the club on a free transfer in the summer of 1957 to become player-manager with Worcester City, a position he later held with Brecon Corinthians and finally Garw Athletic. It was at Worcester that he had perhaps his greatest moments as a manager, when his non-Leaguers knocked out both Millwall and Liverpool in the 1958-59 FA Cup.

For a while after retirement the former miner worked as a lorry driver in his native Rhondda. Unfortunately in more recent times, one of City's most popular – and certainly most inspirational – players suffered from Alzheimer's disease and consequently found it hard to remember his playing days at Maine Road. Many fans fortunately in better health, can certainly remember Roy Paul and what he contributed to the history of Manchester City. Tragically it was this awful ailment that ended Paul's life in May 2002 in a nursing home in Glamorgan. He was 82.

Maine Road career

294 appearances   9 goals

Terry Phelan – genuine pace

SALFORD-BORN Terry Phelan began his footballing career via the not too common route of a YTS scheme with Leeds United in August 1984. Despite his obvious early prowess he managed to play a part in just 15 games for the Yorkshire side before being given a free transfer to Swansea, a side recently relegated to the Fourth Division, in the summer of 1986.

At the same time Leeds released Phelan, they also released another more than capable full-back, and another one who would go to win international honours for the Republic of Ireland. The other player was Dennis Irwin, a man who retired at the end of last season after a glittering career lasting nearly 12 years with Manchester United. Leeds manager at the time Billy Bremner either 'didn't fancy' them or had a surfeit of defenders to choose from. Whatever his reasons for offloading them only seemed to inspire Phelan and Irwin to prove him wrong.

Phelan stayed at Swansea for just the one season before being the subject of a £100,000 transfer fee to Bobby Gould's Wimbledon. It was whilst a member of the infamous 'Crazy Gang' that his career rose to prominence. He was an integral part of the 1988 FA Cup Final side that beat hot favourites Liverpool and following a run of consistent performances, he broke into Jack Charlton's Ireland side for the first time in 1992.

On 24 August that same year he became City's joint record signing when Peter Reid spent £2.5 million, thereby equalling the fee of another former Wimbledon player, Keith Curle. At the time it seemed rather a strange decision. City seemed reasonably well off for defenders (indeed in Neil Pointon they already a very similar player), their current problems stemming more from a lack of goals scored. Wimbledon on the other hand were delighted. Once again they had received a huge sum of money from City, causing some of their fans to gloat that it was only the Blues' apparent generosity that was keeping the Plough Lane outfit going.

Phelan's debut came in the fourth game of the 1992-93 season, a 3-1 victory against Norwich at Maine Road. It was the club's first win of a topsy-turvey season, the first of the newly-formed FA Premier League. It was also a season in which City appeared to favouring the long-ball method of attack, a style of play especially preferred by Reid's number two, Sam Ellis. It was a style not universally popular with Blues' supporters so the sight of Phelan collecting the ball deep inside his own half and setting off on a blistering, mazy run upfield proved a more than welcome diversion. It also enamoured Phelan to the City faithful.

Perhaps the most famous example of one of Phelan's runs came in the quarter-final of the FA Cup against Tottenham. Despite having gone a goal up, City then capitulated and let in four relatively soft goals at the other end. In the dying moments Phelan set off on one of his trademark runs from the back, left untold Spurs defenders in his wake and sidefooted home a truly memorable goal. The crowd, especially those in the newly-opened Umbro Stand behind the goal, simply couldn't believe it and several of them expressed both their delight at the goal and their anger at the result by trespassing on to the pitch.

A left-back with terrific pace, at the height of his career (arguably with City) Phelan was one of the fastest players in the country. He was undoubtedly one of the best attacking full-backs in the game although his fondness to attack did cause concern at the back on occasion. Perhaps the worst example of this came in the 5-0 defeat at Old Trafford in November 1994. So keen was Phelan to get something from the game that his constant rampaging forward only succeeded in giving Andre Kanchelskis the proverbial field day behind him.

He was a regular in the Ireland side during his stay at Maine Road and even played for them in the 1994 World Cup Finals in the United States. After more than 100 games for the Blues he left Maine Road in November 1995 and moved to Chelsea, staying for only a handful of games before moving on to Everton and then Fulham. In the 2001-02 season he was playing alongside Keith Curle again, this time in the colours of Sheffield United.

Terry Phelan was a tough-tackling, no-nonsense full-back who gave his all for Manchester City. Consequently he was loved by the singing hordes on the Kippax.

Maine Road career

121-1 appearances   3 goals

Paul Power – totally committed to the cause

AS a player who played 13 seasons for City it is somewhat ironic that Paul Power's one and only domestic honour should have been won away from Maine Road. In June 1986 manager Billy McNeill surprisingly sold him to Everton for what turned out to be a bargain fee of £75,000. Less than 12 months later Power was the holder of a First Division championship medal and his beloved City had been relegated.

The Openshaw-born Power had been spotted originally as a 12-year-old playing for a Sunday League team called West Park Albion. It was City's tremendous talent seeker Harry Godwin who first noticed the rangy left-footer, one who was equally at home either in midfield or at left-back. Nothing really came of Power's very young days with City but by the time he was 17 Godwin had invited him back again with the promise of games for the A and B teams. Having just been accepted by Leeds University for a degree place studying law, this suited Power perfectly. He could play for the Blues' youngsters at weekends and then travel to and from Leeds so his studies wouldn't be affected. When he helped out his mum and dad running their pub in Salford and with City paying his travelling expenses, Power was unusually well off for a student.

Having signed amateur forms in August 1973 he turned professional two years later. Within a month of signing, the 19-year-old was making his debut in the first team in a 1-0 defeat at Villa Park. It was the first of 436 starts Power would make for City. Only eight men have ever made more. He had 18 starts in all competitions that season, gradually taking over the left-side midfield spot from Alan Oakes, a player who'd seemingly been there almost forever. For the next 10 seasons Paul Power and Manchester City were inseparable.

His tremendous stamina, distribution, tackling and perhaps the most important of all, his commitment to the cause, earned him two Supporters' Clubs Player of the Year awards and, had they been in wider use in those days, the captain's armband for the best part of seven years. Fans really loved to see him doing well and leading out the team, after all, at the end of the day, he'll tell you himself, there is no bigger City fan than Power. During his years as captain he had the honour to lead City out three times at Wembley, the only man ever to do so. Sadly for Power and City, he would never be on a winning side.

He was the ideal team man, one managers could rely on regularly to perform his duties to the best of his abilities. He also contributed a goal or two on occasion, none more so than his spectacular curling free-kick to beat Ipswich Town in the semi-final of the FA Cup in 1981. It was his fifth goal in the competition that season, his year-end total of nine being his best ever in City's colours. Interestingly enough in the season before (the year of Malcolm Allison's return), only Michael Robinson with nine in total, bettered Power's seven.

By the summer of 1986 Power had experienced the devastation of relegation and the joys of promotion. He was also just a few months off his 33rd birthday, by far the longest serving player and had just signed a one-year contract. It was whilst holidaying in Devon that he heard the news not only that Howard Kendall's Everton had shown an interest in him but also Billy McNeill had agreed they could talk to the player.

Expecting to finish his career as purely a squad player, Power moved to only his second (and last) professional club, surprised himself by playing 40 of the 42 League games and picked up his medal. It was a much deserved award and one no City fan would ever begrudge to such a loyal servant. A niggling knee injury finally curtailed his playing days causing him to move on to the coaching side and he looked after both the youngsters and the first team before losing his job in November 1990 thanks to the inevitabilities of a new manager's backroom shake-up. In this case though it was Kendall, the man who'd previously signed him, returning to Goodison Park after two years with Atletico Bilbao.

A man of Power's intelligence and football awareness would not be out of work for long and so it proved. He was offered a job in the Football in the Community programme and later as Coaching Administrator for the PFA. In the summer of 1997 the new man in charge at Maine Road (the fifth in a dreadful five month spell), Frank Clark, made arguably his best decision during his time at Maine Road; he brought Power back to work with the club's junior footballers. Apart from playing, it was the perfect job for Power and one he still holds today.

As a man who gave so much to City in the past, there is no one better qualified to look after its future.

Maine Road career

436-9 appearances   36 goals

Niall Quinn – Ole', ole', ole'

AT 6ft 3ins, Dublin-born Niall Quinn is one of the tallest players to have played for Manchester City. Apart from that, he is also one of its most popular players as well.

During his schooldays in Ireland, Quinn was adept at most ball games. Apart from soccer he also played Gaelic football and hurling and was so good at Australian Rules football that whilst on a school trip to Australia he was offered professional terms by two different clubs. On his return to Ireland he was approached by Arsenal's scout in the Emerald Isle, Bill Darby, who told him he'd been watching him for a while and invited him over to Highbury for a fortnight's trials. Shortly after his 17th birthday (and just a week into his trial) Quinn was offered a three-year contract.

In December 1985 he made his debut for the Gunners in a home game against Liverpool. The tall, gangling centre-forward (weighing all of $9\frac{1}{2}$st) had the best possible start to his professional career by scoring the first goal in his side's 2-0 win. Despite that ideal start, Quinn had a mixed time at Highbury. He played in 35 of the 42 League games of the 1986-87 season, but then managed just 14 starts in the next two and a half years. With stiff competition for places, even by his own admittance, he just 'fell out of favour', a difficult time proving even more frustrating because he was by now a full Irish international and desperate to play.

On 15 March 1990, City manager Howard Kendall offered him the chance of first-team football with a £800,000 transfer. It was just the springboard Quinn needed to secure his place in Jack Charlton's side for the World Cup in Italy later that year. It was also one of the shrewdest signings ever made by Manchester City.

Having scored on his debut for City (against Chelsea) he scored three more times in his nine appearances before leaving for Italy, playing a pivotal role in a side that shocked many during that most memorable of tournaments. His exploits in Italy seemed to spur him on even more for his first full season with the Blues. With Quinn spearheading the attack, City finished the 1990-91 season in fifth place in Division One, their highest position for 12 years. His personal contribution was 22 goals in all competitions (enough to earn him City's Player of the Year award), including a hat-trick against then high flying Crystal Palace. That very same month – April 1991 – was also memorable for two other instances. Just three days before his hat-trick against Palace, Quinn had scored for Ireland in a European championship qualifier at Wembley. Almost three weeks later he saved a penalty from Derby County's Dean Saunders after replacing Tony Coton in goal following the 'keeper's sending-off. Earlier in the same game Quinn had already opened the scoring with a sweetly struck left-foot volley. Like a lot of outfield players Quinn quite fancied himself as a goalkeeper and would even stand between the posts in training, gambling against his teammates to beat him. Not doubt his experiences of handling the ball as a schoolboy all-rounder earned him enough for an occasional flutter on his beloved horses.

For the next three seasons Quinn was a crucial part of City's play, his skill in the air and hold-up play causing ample scoring opportunities for others such as David White and Mike Sheron. However injury was to befall the genial target-man in November 1993 when badly damaged cruciate knee ligaments forced him out of the Irish squad for the World Cup in America. He was back to full fitness for the start of the 1994-95 term although the partnership of Uwe Rosler and Paul Walsh restricted his starts to just 24 in the League while he appeared as substitute on a further 11 occasions.

He finished second behind Rosler in the goalscoring charts of 1995-96, a season that saw the Blues relegated from the Premiership. Not long afterwards, and still with international football on his mind, Quinn moved to Sunderland, joining forces once again with a man who'd earlier been his player-manager at Maine Road, Peter Reid. Even though the latter stages of Quinn's time at Maine Road were spent in the lower echelons of the Premier League, he proved his loyalty to the club by turning down a lucrative move to Sporting Lisbon. It is gestures like this have made Quinn a popular figure not only at clubs for whom he's played.

At the time of writing he is still with Reid at Sunderland, has just enjoyed a testimonial in which all the profits went to charity, and played a part in the Republic of Ireland coming within a penalty shootout of reaching the World Cup quarter-finals in Japan, after which he announced his retirement from international football. He's now 35 and the end of his playing career is closer than the start. It seems likely that after his retirement from playing altogether he will get a job in the media, one that will further enhance his reputation as a genuinely nice guy.

Maine Road career
219-25 appearances   78 goals

Steve Redmond – good enough and old enough

IN April 1986 City's highly talented youth team (seven of the starting line-up would go on to play in the first team) beat neighbours United in the Final of the FA Youth Cup. Captaining the young Blues was central defender Steve Redmond, still only 18 years old and yet a player who had already played in Division One, the Central League, the Full Members' Cup Final at Wembley and in a senior Old Trafford 'derby'.

If he was a mere callow (but powerfully built) youth back in those days, nowadays nothing could be further from the truth. In the 2001-02 season he was assistant manager with Bury, a highly seasoned professional with Premiership experience, and one who still turns out occasionally at the heart of the Shakers' defence. According to their website, staff at Bury are attempting to try and get £10 off him every time one of his clearances leaves the ground! Redmond is still someone who enjoys a laugh and joke (it was he who gave his good mate Ian Brightwell the nickname 'Bob') and probably takes this jest in the obvious good humour it is meant in. What is not known however is whether he has cleared the stand (certainly during his days with City he appeared more than strong enough to do so) and if so, did he ever pay up?

His natural good humour stems from the city of his birth, Liverpool, a city well known for producing some notable comedians and footballers. Born on 2 November 1967, Redmond supported the red side of Stanley Park in his young days and almost joined the Anfield club as a teenager. At the time he was playing for both Liverpool and England Boys but fortunately for City Redmond's father realised his son's chances of furthering his career were at Maine Road, prompting the youngster to sign schoolboy forms in October 1982. Two years later his early promise had persuaded City to offer him professional terms.

His debut in the first team came as a replacement for the injured Kenny Clements on 8 February 1986 in a 2-0 home win against Queen's Park Rangers. He played nine League games in his debut season, really establishing himself next time out, playing 30 times in a poor season, one that ultimately resulted in relegation.

New manager Mel Machin came on board for the start of the 1987-88 season and immediately awarded the captaincy to the 19-year-old. Redmond had become City's youngest ever captain and thanked Machin in the best way possible; he was an ever present for the next two seasons. For one so young he commanded respect from the more senior players around him and his performances at the heart of City's defence gave the fans hope that the club had indeed discovered a player genuinely felt to be 'one for the future'. At the end of his first season as captain he was voted Player of the Year, an award richly deserved following a season of fine performances from this calm, cultured and solid defender. At the end of his second season as captain, the Blues had won promotion back to the top flight.

He continued to be a regular in the side and captain for the next two years up until record signing Keith Curle's arrival, one that almost immediately took away his captain's responsibilities and would eventually see him on his way to Oldham Athletic. Curiously enough the last two seasons Redmond played at Maine Road had seen City finish on both occasions in fifth place in the First Division. It appeared that as far as the defence was concerned, the Blues seemed to have their house in order.

On 5 August 1992, still only 24 and a veteran of more than 280 League and Cup games, Redmond moved to Boundary Park with teammate Neil Pointon in a deal that brought winger Rick Holden to Maine Road. With hindsight it was not the greatest exchange deal ever. His transfer to Oldham meant that Redmond never had the opportunity to play for City in the newly-formed Premier League, a feat he did manage for two years with Latics.

Steve Redmond made a huge impact at a remarkably early age for City and yet arguably his prime playing years were spent at (and with all due respect) lesser and smaller clubs. Had he stayed, it is pure speculation that he would have added to his collection of England Youth and Under 21 caps. Perhaps in the end he was very similar to Tommy Caton, a man who also promised so much in his early days but never seemed to be able to take the next step forward. Still, it was fun while it lasted.

Maine Road career

283-4 appearances   7 goals

Nicky Reid – not all the judgements were wrong

ON 7 March 1979, City played Borussia Mönchengladbach in what was to date, their penultimate European tie. The UEFA Cup game at Maine Road finished 1-1 and saw the debut in the first team of an 18-year-old who, apart from a handful of appearances in the reserves, was primarily still an A team player.

That player was Davyhulme-born Nicky Reid, a relatively small, tenacious and solidly built defender and one who would go to play more than 250 games for the club. He was another example of many up and coming young players the club's excellent scouting system was producing at the time. Despite a considerable amount of criticism against the returning Malcolm Allison's policies, his judgement of the benefits of playing youngsters such as Reid and Tommy Caton proved spot on. Reid took to senior football like the proverbial duck to water. Just two years after his debut, he was playing in front of 100,000 in an FA Cup Final. He'd come a long way since his days with Whitehall Juniors.

Reid had initially signed for City on 30 April 1977, turning professional on 30 October the following year, his 18th birthday. His first appearance in the League came three weeks after that game with Mönchengladbach, a 2-1 defeat at Ipswich, although in between times, he had played in the return leg in Germany. In his debut season he made 10 appearances (one as a substitute) taking Ray Ranson's place at right-back.

On Boxing Day 1979 he played in a 1-1 home draw with Stoke. He missed just one of the remaining 19 League games that season and proved to be a highly accomplished defender, equally at home as a full-back or in the centre of defence and established himself firmly in the side. With successful runs in both the FA and League Cups of 1980-81, Reid played 51 games in total, a figure that meant he'd played more than 80 games for the Blues and still not yet reached his 21st birthday. His abilities had not gone unnoticed by England either and he had won six under 21 caps by the time he did 'become of age'.

Under new manager John Bond, Reid had played in the back four against Tottenham in both games of the 100th FA Cup Final of 1981 but found himself moved to midfield when the manager's son Kevin arrived at the start of the following season. He was initially unable to settle in his new role and appeared out of sorts but the support of the fans coupled with the player's own mental strength pulled him through this difficult transition period. Perhaps as an aid to the player, he was allowed to join NASL side Seattle Sounders for a five-month loan spell in 1982.

Once back in England Reid regained his place in the side and continued his efforts in the Blues' midfield, suffering both the disappointment of relegation against Luton in 1983 and the joys of promotion two years later although he missed out through injury on the final day against Charlton. At this point he was averaging 36 games a season over the last six and promotion was just reward for his efforts.

Never noted for his goalscoring abilities, Reid's only two senior goals for City both came in the space of three weeks of the 1983-84 season. On 11 February he scored in a 2-1 win against Portsmouth then on 3 March his was the only goal of the game at Maine Road against Shrewsbury.

In July 1987, more than 10 years after he'd first put pen to paper at Maine Road, Reid moved to Blackburn Rovers on a free transfer. He was still only 27 and played more than 170 League games for the Ewood Park side over the next five years. He then had a loan spell at Bristol City before signing for West Bromwich Albion, later turning out for Wycombe Wanderers, Bury and Witton Albion. Moving into management, Reid took the Irish side Sligo Rovers to success in their League Cup in 1997-98.

Nicky Reid is a fine example of the old adage, "If they're good enough, they're old enough."

Maine Road career

256-6 appearances   2 goals

Peter Reid – a leader by example

ONE of the most genuine and honest players English football has ever seen, Peter Reid himself will admit that when he arrived at Maine Road on a free transfer from Queen's Park Rangers on 12 December 1989 his best playing days were behind him. Even so he still became an inspiration to City both as a fearless, tough-tackling midfielder and later as manager.

Born in Huyton in June 1956, Reid's boyhood club was Everton, a club he'd later win both domestic and European honours with. And yet, despite training with the Merseysiders as a teenager, then manager Harry Catterick failed to sign him and so Reid moved to Bolton. Once established in the Bolton side he became an almost permanent fixture, missing just four games in a three and a half year spell in the mid-1970s, collecting a Second Division championship winners' medal in 1978.

Not surprisingly, the ever-aggressive Reid has suffered his fair share of playing injuries. These include breaks to left knee and right leg and tears to right knee ligaments and left knee cartilage. Because of these long-term setbacks many felt his playing days were over, many that is except Everton, the club that had previously released him. In December 1982 he moved back to his native Liverpool for a bargain fee of £60,000; he'd played more than 200 League games for Bolton, scoring 23 times.

It was at Goodison that Reid's reputation was built. For the next six years he was at the heart of an Everton side that won the League championship twice, the FA Cup, the European Cup-winners' Cup and was a runner-up on three other occasions at Wembley. During that time he also voted the PFA Player of the Year, won all 13 of his England caps and took part in the Mexico World Cup of 1986, in particular the game against Maradona's Argentina, 'Hand of God' and all. Regretably even the tigerish Reid failed to stop the brilliant Argentinean's second goal; if only his legs had been as quick as his mind, the greatest con-man of them all wouldn't have got five yards into his magical run. In February 1989 the 32-year-old found himself surplus to requirements to Colin Harvey's side and moved south on a free transfer for a 10-month spell with Queen's Park Rangers.

When Howard Kendall took over the managerial reigns at Maine Road in December 1989 he decided almost instantly that the Blues needed more steel and resolve and felt certain that the best place to acquire such necessary raw material was at his old hunting ground. In Peter Reid there was no better example of what Kendall was looking for.

City fans took to Reid almost instantly. His combative instinct and terrible dislike of losing heartened Blues' followers, all of whom will gladly give their devotion to players who wear the famous sky-blue shirt with pride. He was also hugely popular with his teammates, a fact that would ultimately go towards his sudden departure from Maine Road nearly four years later. Reid's title initially was player-coach, one he kept for just on a year until his old mentor Kendall soured himself forever with City fans when he returned to his first love, Goodison Park.

Mortified by the sudden departure of Kendall, Blues' supporters longed for some consistency in the manager's chair and Peter Reid seemed the obvious choice to carry on Kendall's early work and indeed improve on it. Chairman Peter Swales made Reid City's first-ever player-manager although by the time Steve McMahon arrived the following Christmas, Reid had almost given up on the playing side to concentrate fully on managing the team.

Under Reid City played some of their best football seen in a long time; back-to-back top 10 positions in the Premiership confirm this. With David White and Niall Quinn leading a most potent attacking force, perhaps Reid's only downside as City manager (apart from his parting of the ways with many popular and experienced City backroom staff) was the sometimes over-used long-ball method, a style of play many put down to his number two Sam Ellis rather than to Reid himself.

The 1994-95 season started badly for City. Without a win in their first four games, fans nevertheless were shocked again when the likeable Scouser was unceremoniously sacked. After two of the best seasons in a long time, four games didn't seem that long a period to correct what ever it was that apparently had gone wrong so quickly. On a non-contract basis Reid played a combined total of 13 League games for Southampton, Notts. County and Bury (where he also did some coaching) before taking over as manager of Sunderland in March 1995.

Maine Road career
100-14 appearances   2 goals

Don Revie – always in space, always had time

AS a player Don Revie was an FA Cup winner with City, represented the Football League, played for England 'B' and was capped six times for his country at full international level. And yet despite his successes on the pitch it is as manager of Leeds United that he will probably be best remembered.

Born in Middlesbrough in July 1927, Revie played for local sides Archibald Road School, Newport Boys' Club and Middlesbrough Swifts before joining Leicester in August 1944. The former apprentice bricklayer played more than 100 times for the Filbert Street side and was desperately unlucky not to play in the 1949 FA Cup Final when a ruptured blood vessel in his nose put him out of action.

Not long after that missed Final, Revie was linked with Hull City and Arsenal, and even visited Maine Road to see what Manchester City could offer him. In the end he turned down Jock Thomson's offer and joined Hull in November. Two years later he changed his mind, the subject of a £25,000 deal by new manager Les McDowall, a deal that included Ernie Phillips moving to Yorkshire. He was a regular in the City sides of the early 1950s, however these were lean times for the Blues who languished too near the bottom of the First Division for comfort. In later years Revie himself wondered whether he'd made a wise choice after all in moving to Maine Road. Things would change for both club and player in 1954, they year of the brilliant Hungarian destruction of England at Wembley.

Les McDowall had witnessed the Hungarian's method of employing a deep-lying centre-forward, a position at the time unknown in England, and one that confused the centre-halves of the day who didn't know whether to stay where they were or go in search of the strolling attacker. The hope was that the defender would leave his position at the back thereby creating gaps that the inside-forwards could exploit. McDowall tried this plan initially in the reserves with Johnny Williamson at centre-forward and it worked so well that Revie was asked to try it out in the first team. Initially it wasn't a great success but when Ken Barnes was promoted from the reserves, his partnership with Revie worked beautifully and surprised defences up and down the country. This style of play became known as the Revie Plan, even though the player himself would admit that although instrumental in its success, it wasn't his idea.

Playing this way took the Blues to two successive FA Cup Finals in 1955 and 1956, although being reduced to 10 men against Newcastle effectively disrupted this revolutionary new style. With a full team the following year the plan worked brilliantly, Revie's superb passing dissecting the Birmingham defence to help the Blues gain a 3-1 victory. However successful the plan worked Revie was not always at the heart of it. He had more than the occasional disagreement with McDowall and was set to miss the 1956 Final right up until midday of the game itself when Billy Spurdle suffered an outbreak of boils, a misfortune that meant Revie was in the starting line-up for only his second Cup game of the season.

For all his thinking and ability he was awarded the Footballer of the Year trophy in 1955 thereby becoming the first City player to achieve that accolade.

Less than six months after the Wembley triumph against Newcastle, Revie moved back to his native north-east when a £21,500 move took him to Sunderland. He stayed with the Wearsiders for two years before joining Leeds United as player-manager in March 1961. In May 1963 he retired from playing and set about building a formidable Leeds side, one that was successful in both domestic and European competitions. Curiously enough the physical style of play Leeds adopted was in stark contrast to the more cultured way Revie himself played at City. It undoubtedly increased Leeds' team spirit although failed to win many admirers outside of Yorkshire.

When Joe Mercer finished his stint as caretaker manager of the England side in the summer of 1974, Don Revie seemed his most logical replacement. Although honoured by the position, Revie missed the everyday contact with his players and consequently was never really happy in his new job. In July 1977 he shocked both supporters and the establishment by accepting a reported £60,000 a year job coaching the United Arab Emirates national side. After three years in the UAE he took up a similar post in Egypt, one that proved to be his last in the game. In his late 50s, Revie became a victim of motor neurone disease, a tragic affliction that would ultimately cause his death, in Edinburgh, on 26 May 1989. He was 61.

Maine Road career

178 appearances   41 goals

Frank Roberts – goalscorer supreme

INSIDE-RIGHT Frank Roberts has the misfortune to be recorded in the history books as the player who missed the first-ever penalty at Maine Road. Gough in the Sheffield United goal saved his spot-kick on that opening day back in August 1923 although the miss doesn't appear to have weighed too heavily on his mind. In seven seasons with City, Roberts averaged better than a goal every other game, a strike rate that makes him the tenth leading goalscorer in the club's history.

The Sandbach-born forward was 28 when he joined the Blues from Bolton Wanderers on 18 October 1922, his fee of £3,400 being high for the time but raising even more eyebrows when his age was also taken into consideration. Many thought it was far too much although when he played every game for the rest of the 1922-23 season (the last one at Hyde Road), scoring 10 times along the way, the majority of those doubters had altered their opinion. Along with Horace Barnes and Tommy Johnson, Roberts became part of a potent City forward line with Roberts himself top scoring in three out of four consecutive seasons.

His most prolific outing was 1924-25 when he scored 31 of City's total of 76 in the League. His nearest challenger was Johnson with 12. This tally included four against Liverpool and a hat-trick against Sheffield United, examples of the kind of firepower that earned him the first of his four England caps against Belgium in 1924.

With Roberts once again leading the way the following term, City went all the way to Wembley only to lose 1-0 to Bolton Wanderers in the FA Cup Final. Roberts scored nine goals during that Cup run including five in an amazing 11-4 win against Crystal Palace in the fifth round. To date Roberts is one of only two City players (the other being Bobby Marshall against Swindon Town in 1930) who've achieved this feat in a completed FA Cup tie.

Following David Ashworth's departure in November, City were managerless for most of that particular season and perhaps not surprisingly their League performances stuttered throughout. They failed to match their Cup form and the Blues were duly relegated the week after the Cup Final; the highest point in the League being the 6-1 win at Old Trafford when Roberts found the net twice in the first-half.

In May 1928 City were crowned champions of the Second Division, a success that would provide Roberts with his only domestic honour. Apart from winning the title it proved another remarkable season for both player and club. With 20 in total (all in the League), Roberts shared the top spot with Johnson (19 in the League and one in the Cup), City scored exactly one hundred in the League (they'd managed 108 the year before) and an average home crowd of 37,458 watched the Blues in action. It was the highest in any of the four Divisions.

Roberts played 15 times during the 1928-29 season, his lowest turnout since joining the club. By now he was 35, Johnson as well as recent arrivals Eric Brook and Freddie Tilson were proving to be more prolific in front of goal and so Roberts' days seemed to be numbered. On 14 June 1929 he was transferred to Manchester Central before finishing his career with Horwich RMI.

Frank Roberts' knack of being in the right place at the right time earned him the reputation of being one of the finest attacking players of his generation and his goalscoring achievements made him a hugely popular figure amongst City supporters of the 1920s. Even today City fans love an out and out goalscorer; just look at the praise and adulation heaped on Shaun Goater.

I wonder what they fed Roberts on back in the days of rough, heavy boots and even rougher, heavier balls? Whatever it was it most certainly worked.

Hyde Road-Maine Road career

237 appearances   130 goals

Uwe Rosler – City's German bomber

IT made a great slogan and looked good on the tee-shirts of the time but Uwe Rosler's grandfather did not bomb Old Trafford; he was in the German navy. However it has been recorded by at least one eminent City historian that Rosler liked the tee-shirts so much he even bought one for his aforementioned grandfather! The young Rosler though certainly bombed a few opposition goalmouths (and broke more than a few good maiden's hearts) during his time with City. He was without question one of the most popular players of recent, or for that matter, any other times. His goal celebrations gave the impression that in return, he loved the fans almost as much as they loved him.

Born in Attenburg in what was then East Germany, on 15 November 1968, Rosler first appeared at Maine Road on loan shortly before the transfer deadline in March 1994. He'd apparently previously failed to impress Middlesbrough during a two-week trial in the north-east but had no such difficulty with Blues' boss Brian Horton. Following his debut at Queen's Park Rangers on 5 March (where his back-heel set up the equaliser by David Rocastle) Rosler played in the remaining 11 games, scoring five times, including three in the last four outings. Horton and City had seen enough. On 1 June the Blues paid Rosler's Bundesliga club, FC Nurnberg, £375,000 for his services on a permanent basis, a proverbial bargain for an international centre-forward, one who had been already been capped 10 times by East Germany. In fact so successful was Rosler at Maine Road that he even outshone his much more lauded countryman Jurgen Klinsmann, at the time plying his trade at Tottenham.

In his first full season he topped the goalscoring charts with 22 in all competitions, a figure that included four in a League Cup game against Notts. County. Coupled with his goals was also a tremendous battling quality and a never say die attitude, three features that when combined, were enough to earn him the club's Player of the Year Trophy. It proved to be the first of three successive seasons that saw Rosler lead the way in the goalscoring charts. He seemed to be at his best when playing alongside his great friend Paul Walsh, a diminutive forward who'd joined City from Portsmouth in the same month as Rosler. With Summerbee and Beagrie providing a steady supply of crosses from both wings, their partnership helped to brighten up otherwise lacklustre showings during what were uncertain times at Maine Road.

When Alan Ball replaced Horton as manager, Rosler's performances, and consequently his goal tally, seemed to suffer, a complaint allegedly fuelled by an apparent lack of harmony between the striker and the World Cup winner. Having been dropped to the substitutes' bench for the Maine Road 'derby', when finally called on he scored a fine solo goal just a few minutes into the action. His race to the dug-out and subsequent gestures to Ball seemed to prove that the always-emotional Rosler had a point, whatever it might have been.

Even though the Blues were relegated shortly after that game with United, Rosler put the events of a disappointing season behind him and stayed loyal to the club. Despite his best efforts (15 goals in 44 outings) no one else, with the exception of Georgi Kinkladze, contributed anything to a poor campaign, one that promised so much at the start (City were favourites for promotion) but ended in 14th place. Things got worse the following year. New record signing Lee Bradbury restricted Rosler's appearances and the Blues were relegated to the Second (technically Third) Division, the lowest they'd ever been. Just before the final nails had been driven into the Blues' coffin, Rosler returned to his homeland to join Kaiserslautern, a team topping the Bundesliga at the time. 12 months later he was on the move again, this time to Tennis Borussia Berlin, a team that would find itself bankrupt in May 2000.

Rosler has always said the four years he spent at City were the most enjoyable of his career and he loved living in England. Finding himself out of work in Berlin he decided to try and find a way back to these shores and joined Southampton in the summer. Injuries and a loss of form combined to make his 18 months on the south coast far from happy and he was last seen on loan in West Bromwich Albion's colours in the 2001-02 season.

Uwe Rosler's career at Maine Road coincided with arguably the most disruptive period in the club's history. A succession of managers (who brought a seemingly never ending bunch of new players with them), relegations and even the overthrow of the existing chairman made any kind of consistency on the pitch virtually impossible. Had it not been for the tireless efforts of the German Bomber, things could conceivably have been worse.

Maine Road career
165-12 appearances   64 goals

Joe Royle – too much too soon?

JOE Royle's reputation in professional football is second to none. After a playing career spanning some 18 years (including six England caps) he began a managerial career lasting slightly longer. At the time of writing, the jovial Liverpudlian is currently out of work professionally although is still much sought after as a television pundit. A man who speaks both his mind and a great deal of common sense has been linked with various jobs since leaving City in May 2001; it will be a great waste of talent and experience if the situation is not altered sooner rather than later.

His playing days began at Everton as an apprentice in July 1964, turning professional two years later. With a 6ft 1ins frame and weighing the best part of 14st, Royle had the perfect physique for the traditional English centre-forward. Having made his debut in the Everton first team as a 16-year-old, he used his powerful frame to become one of the game's best headers of the ball, an attribute that provided many of his 102 League goals for the Toffees.

On Christmas Eve 1974, Royle had successfully recovered fully from a back operation but was unable to find a way back into Everton's first team. Several clubs showed an interest in signing him but City boss Tony Book held off their challenges and persuaded him (although he himself admits to needing very little persuading – he agreed a deal within an hour!) to come to Maine Road. It proved a great deal for both player and club.

Playing alongside the likes of Summerbee, Bell, Marsh, Hartford and Tueart, Royle could only manage one goal in 16 League games in his debut season but really came into his own the following one. That was 1975-76, a season that saw only Dennis Tueart (with 24) score more than Royle's 18 as the Blues went on to lift the League Cup with a 2-1 triumph over Newcastle United. Royle scored in every round of the competition that term and was disappointed not to make it a memorable collection in the Final itself when what looked like a perfectly good chip was ruled out for offside. He averaged a goal in every four games for City, not the most prolific ratio for a centre-forward, but Tueart and later Brian Kidd, were more than grateful for his knock downs and the way he generally upset oppositions' defences.

After leaving Maine Road in November 1977 he played exactly one hundred League games (plus one as substitute) for Bristol City before a knee injury ended his playing days whilst in the colours of Norwich in 1982, an injury that probably set the 33-year-old on the managerial path earlier than he would have predicted.

Less than three months after retiring, he was back in his native north-west, in the manager's chair at Second Division Oldham. Amazingly he was in charge at Boundary Park for 12 years, during which time (and perhaps not too surprisingly) he became the League's longest-serving manager. On the proverbial shoestring, Royle literally did perform miracles with Oldham. In 1991 they won the Second Division championship, a triumph that meant they'd returned to the top division for the first time in 68 years. The previous year Oldham had reached the semi-final of the FA Cup (losing to eventual winners Manchester United after a replay) and then the Final of the League Cup only to lose by a solitary goal to Brian Clough's Nottingham Forest. During these halcyon days, he was even offered the manager's job at Maine Road but, to the delight of the Latics' fans, he declined Peter Swales' offer.

In October 1994 he was finally tempted away from Oldham and returned to Goodison Park, guiding Everton to a FA Cup win just a few months later. His managerial time with Everton lasted until the spring of 1997 when he was sacked, a dismissal that began a year out of the game until, in February 1998, he was yet again linked again with the 'hot seat' at Maine Road. This time though he accepted Francis Lee's offer but despite having 15 games left to turn things around was unable to prevent the Blues slipping into what was really the third tier of English football for the first time in their history.

The 1998-99 season – the one Royle himself described as 'horrible' – culminated in the amazing play-off win against Gillingham. With the nucleus of the Second Division side, Royle began an assault on the First Division. Remarkably he gained back-to-back promotions.

Regretably though the bubble had to burst eventually and when it did it ultimately cost Royle his job. After just one season in the Premiership, the Blues once again found themselves relegated. Had it been simply a case of too much too soon? Having said that though, would anyone connected with any football club let alone Manchester City, turn down the opportunity to play in the Premiership? I think the simple answer is no.

Maine Road career

124-2 appearances   32 goals

Cliff Sear – style, culture and a great sliding tackle

LEFT-BACK Cliff Sear was probably the last in a long line of former miners who gave up their jobs working hours below ground to play football for Manchester City.

He was born in Rhostyllen near Wrexham in September 1936 and it was whilst working at Bershaw Colliery that he first attracted City's attentions. He signed amateur forms for the Blues in June 1955, still working five days a week down the pit and travelling to Manchester every Saturday to play for the B team. Although he played most weekends, even by his own admission, he felt his playing career had come to a halt and he had achieved all he was ever going to at Maine Road. These thoughts when coupled with the inconveniences and costs involved travelling every week caused the elegant defender to change his outlook and he joined Cheshire League side Oswestry Town.

Ironically it was whilst playing for Oswestry that manager Les McDowall spotted him and thought he could do a good job as a professional for City. So, on 4 January 1957, some 18 months after they'd had him as an amateur, City bought him for £1,750. Over the next 9 years Sear played nearly 280 times for the Blues so in the end it proved to be money very well spent.

He made his debut in the last game of the 1956-57 season (a 3-3 draw at Birmingham) but established himself next time out, playing 29 League games as a replacement for Wembley winner Roy Little. Sear's time at Maine Road coincided with the gradual break up of that successful 1956 FA Cup Final team and the arrival of Joe Mercer and Malcolm Allison in the summer of 1965. Not surprisingly this interim period proved a very difficult one for City. Had it not been for Sear at the back though things could have been considerably worse.

He always seemed to have time on the ball, was very stylish in all he did and he possessed as good a sliding tackle as had ever been seen at Maine Road. His cultured performances in a City shirt earned him two Welsh Under-23 caps and one full cap, against England at Wembley in 1962. Unfortunately for Sear he was in a side beaten 4-0. He suffered a further disappointment later that same season when City were relegated despite all his efforts.

For the following two seasons – the last two under George Poyser's command – Sear vied for the number three jersey with Vic Gomersall. He played 19 League games in the successful 1965-66 season, one that proved doubly pleasing for the player as City won the Second Division championship and (against Bolton Wanderers) he scored his one and only senior goal for the Blues. However as Mercer and Allison tried to secure a place once again in the top division, that season proved to be Sear's last in the first team.

As Glyn Pardoe steadily improved and Sear entered his 30s it seemed only a matter of time before the willowy Welshman would be moving on. That time finally arrived in April 1968 when he joined Chester. After a further 49 League appearances he eventually retired from playing and started a variety of backroom jobs that would keep him at Sealand Road until 1991 when he was offered the position of Youth Development Officer at Wrexham. At Chester he was number two for a while to another former Blue Alan Oakes, manager himself when Oakes was sacked in 1982 and later youth team coach. It was as youth team coach that he developed the obvious potential of a certain Ian Rush. He continued working with the game's up and coming young players throughout the 1990s at Wrexham and was rewarded for his efforts with a testimonial game in May 1996. The opposition was Manchester City who lost 6-1 to Wrexham in front of nearly 4,000.

Reginald Clifford Sear was a man who always wanted to put something back into the game he loved so much and had employed him in one capacity or another for more than 40 years. His death from a heart attack on 12 July 2000 shocked everyone who knew and respected him. He was 63.

Maine Road career

279 appearances   1 goal

Bert Sproston – "Isn't he on the wrong side?"

WHEN Bert Sproston travelled north to Maine Road with Tottenham Hotspur on Friday, 4 November 1938, few people could have known what was in store for him over the next 24 hours. When the game kicked off at 3 o'clock on the Saturday, Sproston took up his usual place at right-back, only he was now in City's colours!

Sproston was born in Elworth near the Cheshire town of Sandbach on 22 June 1915. After impressing in local football with Sandbach Ramblers, he was offered trials by both Huddersfield Town and Leeds United, deciding on a move to Leeds as a 17-year-old. Once established in the first team at Elland Road, he played 130 League games in five years as well as becoming an England international. One of the 11 caps he won was awarded for his part in the 6-3 win against Germany in Berlin 1938, a famous game remembered for the England players being forced to give the Nazi salute prior to kick-off.

Somewhat surprisingly (rumours suggest it was a financial necessity) Leeds sold him to Tottenham few weeks after that game in Berlin. Being a real northerner, Sproston found the hustle and bustle of the capital too much for him and he struggled to settle at his new club. His tenth game for Spurs would have been at Maine Road but the intervening transfer fee of £10,500 prevented him from reaching double figures. Incidentally that game also saw Eric Westwood's first appearance for the Blues and thanks to goals from the returning Doherty and Milsom, both new boys finished on the winning side. Sproston's new salary at Maine Road was £10 a week if the Blues won and £8 a week if they lost. It was one of the highest salaries in the game at that particular time. His transfer fee was also the highest until that point for a defender.

Regretably Sproston was denied a true City career by the outbreak of World War Two. He spent time serving with the British army in India but was also able to turn out for the Blues in more than 70 wartime games. The never hurried and tough-tackling full-back won two wartime England caps, against Wales at Cardiff in 1940 and Scotland at Hampden Park the following year. The player himself later recalled the Nazi propaganda broadcaster Lord Haw Haw telling the Scots he 'hoped they liked the first-half, because Hampden was going to be bombed in the second-half'. It didn't stop 75,000 turning up for the game, but, just to be on the safe side, RAF fighters circled high above the stadium for the game's entirety.

After the war Sproston was a regular in the City side. His full-back partner for the last couple of seasons was Eric Westwood his fellow debutant and another defender who took no prisoners. In 1946-47 (the first full season after the war had ended) City were watched eagerly by an average of more than 39,000 at Maine Road, won 17 of their 21 home League games and finished as Second Division champions. Along with George Smith, Sproston played in 38 League games (more than any other player) and collected what was to be his only medal with the club.

He retired from the game in the 1950 close season although he did turn out occasionally afterwards as an amateur with Ashton National. In July 1951 Bolton Wanderers employed him, firstly as a physiotherapist-coach and latterly as a scout. Sproston was 84 when he passed away in February 2000.

Maine Road career

131 appearances   5 goals   (not including wartime games)

Mike Summerbee – "I wouldn't last a half today!"

BY his own admittance, Mike Summerbee would struggle to finish a whole game today. His hard and aggressive (and yet by no means 'dirty') style of play made him a Maine Road favourite for 10 years but would not be tolerated by today's referees. Neither too would they tolerate the way he used to talk back to them or drop his shorts to the opposition's supporters!

Although born in Preston (where his father George played professionally) Summerbee grew up in the West Country and his performances for non-League side Cheltenham were enough to bring him to the attention of then Third Division Swindon Town. After making his debut in 1959, Summerbee went on play more than 200 League games for Swindon, scoring 39 times, and was a member of the side that won promotion to the Second Division in 1963. In January 1965 he played and scored for Swindon when they beat City at Maine Road in front of a crowd of 8,015, the Blues' lowest ever attendance for a League match.

By the start of the following season, 1965-66, Mike Summerbee was a Manchester City player. Signed by new manager Joe Mercer for just £35,000, Summerbee made his debut in the opening game at Middlesbrough and played in every one of the 52 League and Cup games that term. At the end of the season Summerbee had collected another medal and City had been promoted. Over the next few years, Summerbee's name was one of the first to be penciled in on the team sheet as City collected trophy after trophy, both domestic and European. Possibly the lowest point of his career was when he broke a leg in the League Cup Final against West Bromwich Albion, an injury that forced him the miss the European Cup-winners' Cup Final in Vienna a few weeks later.

Equally at home at either centre-forward or out on the right-wing, Summerbee also won eight England caps during his time at Maine Road. He made his full international debut in the red-hot cauldron of Hampden Park in February 1968 during a 1-1 draw. The little matter of 100,000 plus screaming Scots only flamed Summerbee's will to win even more. Like he's always said, "Fans never call a bad player."

Not necessarily known as a goalscorer, Summerbee was more than capable of finding the net on occasion. Those who saw his goal at St James's Park in the championship decider and his stunning last-minute equaliser in a 3-3 draw with Manchester United still remember them with huge smiles on their faces. No City fan could ever forget either him following up Francis Lee's indirect free-kick to silence a stunned Stretford End and send City to Wembley and the 1970 League Cup Final.

In July 1975 Summerbee moved to Lancashire neighbours Burnley for £25,000; incredibly his 10 superb years of service at Maine Road had cost just £1,000 per season. During his time at Maine Road the always fashion conscious 'Buzzer' had been a boutique owner (with his great friend George Best) and built up a bespoke shirt making business, one which he still runs today. After Burnley, Summerbee joined Blackpool before finishing his career as player-manager with Stockport County where, using his many contacts made whilst with City, he managed to get (amongst other things) a complete new kit and the changing rooms redecorated all for nothing!

His brief flirtation with Hollywood has been much chronicled and maligned, although the movie *Escape to Victory* did mean he could add both Michael Caine and Sylvester Stallone to an already impressive list of shirt-buying clientele.

Mike's son, Nicky, signed for the Blues in the summer of 1994, also from Swindon, a move that obviously meant comparisons with his illustrious father. Mike never interfered with his son's footballing career and despite lots of (most of the time) totally uncalled for abuse and criticism, Nicky played more than 150 games in three years before being sold to Sunderland. When Nicky made his debut for Swindon in 1989 it meant three generations of Summerbee's had played first-class football in England, the first time this feat had ever been achieved.

A long-standing friend of Francis Lee, Summerbee became a supporter of his former teammate during Lee's Maine Road takeover bid in the early 1990s. Using the financial acumen gleaned from his own business ventures, he is today putting it to good use working for the club's corporate division on the sales side, a position that finds him at Maine Road on most days of the week. Even today, some 20 years since he last played for the club, Summerbee is still hugely popular with City fans.

Maine Road career

449-3 appearances   68 goals

Frank Swift – hands 'like frying pans'

NOT only was Frank Swift one of the greatest goalkeepers the world has ever seen, he was also one of the game's greatest characters. His ability to catch long-range shots with one enormous hand – and then throw the ball out easily to the halfway line to start a City attack – was matched equally by his ability to keep his teammates amused with hilarious impressions.

Standing at 6ft 2ins and weighing in at over 13st, Swift was born in Blackpool on 26 December 1913 and plied his trade firstly with that town's Gas Work's side before moving to Fleetwood. It was from Fleetwood that he signed for City as an amateur in October 1932. Just over three weeks later he'd turned professional. After only five reserve games Swift made his debut in City's first team on Christmas Day 1933 although it was hardly an auspicious start. He had to pick the ball out his net four times in Derby County's victory at the Baseball Ground. Only Ernie Toseland provided any festive joy for the Blues with a consolation goal that day. Things had been considerably worse for City just two days prior to Swift's debut; they'd lost 8-0 at Molineux.

Even though he hadn't made the best of starts Swift played in the remaining 21 League games that season. Amazingly up until the outbreak of World War Two in September 1939 – more than five and a half years and 231 games after his debut – Swift missed just one League match for the Blues. During that time he'd been to two consecutive FA Cup Finals at Wembley, a spectator in 1933 as City lost to Everton but a player – and winner – 12 months later against Portsmouth. It was a fantastic end to his debut season. On hearing the final whistle that day Swift fainted between the posts with relief and emotion. "What a daft thing for a big fella like me to do," he later said.

Swift's ability soon brought attention from the England selectors and he won 15 of his 19 caps before war broke out. He tried manfully to 'do his bit' for the war effort but by his own admittance was useless as a traffic policeman and gave the job up on his first day. Like countless others Swift lost his best playing years to the hostilities although he did still play over 130 times for the Blues during that time as well as 14 games for the national side. He had possibly his greatest moment in October 1943 when in goal for England, he stood back and admired an 8-0 thrashing of 'the auld enemy' Scotland. What made it even more pleasurable was the game was played in front of his home supporters at Maine Road. In May 1948 Swift captained England in a 4-0 win against Italy in Turin making him the first goalkeeper to do so.

When the 1949-50 season started, Swift, at 35, knew he was close to retirement. The board had other ideas though and tried desperately to persuade him to stay on. In the end it was no good and he played just four games before finally retiring in September. Two months later another magnificent goalkeeper would take his place in the side; a former German paratrooper called Bert Trautmann. Even today senior Blues' followers still discuss which of the two was best.

After retirement Swift tried his hand unsuccessfully in the catering business for a short while before turning his hand to journalism. He was so well liked and respected by everyone in the game that he made this transition easily and would often be seen covering matches involving neighbours Manchester United, no doubt reminiscing with his old teammate Matt Busby. Whilst working for the *News of the World* in February 1958 he was asked to cover United's European Cup tie in Belgrade. Even though Swift did admit to not particularly liking flying, he still made the trip, one that would end in tragic circumstances on a snow-covered Munich runway on the return journey. One of the greatest goalkeepers the world has ever seen and a man genuinely liked by supporters of all teams lost his life just six weeks after celebrating his 44th birthday.

Maine Road career

376 appearances   (not including wartime games)

Fred Tilson – nothing to worry about

NOT unlike Johnny Hart 25 years later, Fred Tilson was the unfortunate victim of injury and illness which combined to shorten what was undoubtedly a terrific Maine Road career.

He arrived in Manchester in March 1928 along with his Barnsley teammate Eric Brook, the subject of a combined fee of £6,000. Both players had already made reputations for themselves as exciting partners on the left-wing for the Yorkshire side and they continued to perform in the same vein in City's colours. His debut came in a 2-0 win over Grimsby Town, the first of six appearances in what proved to be a Second Division championship season.

With 12 goals in 22 games the following season, Tilson appeared to be establishing himself in the side, particularly towards the end of the campaign. By August 1929 he'd become first choice inside-left and after playing in each of the first six games, he travelled to Old Trafford in readiness for the eighth game of the 1929-30 season. It was a bitter sweet day for Tilson; City won 3-1 but he received a bad leg injury, one so serious he played just three more games in the remainder of that season.

Tilson really came into his own in the early 1930s. On their way to reaching the FA Cup semi-final in 1932, the Blues beat Brentford 6-1 thanks largely to Tilson's hat-trick. His total of 16 goals was bettered (and doubled) by David Halliday and he scored in six out of eight League games leading up to Christmas. Next time out City reached Wembley (only to lose 3-0 to Everton) with Tilson scoring six times, including a hat-trick in the 9-0 defeat of Gateshead. Had he not been injured in a goalless draw with Leeds less than a month before the Final, then perhaps the Merseysiders would have found things a little differently on that April day. With Halliday seemingly falling out of favour, only Brook with 21 came close to top scorer Tilson's 23 that year.

Again plagued by a series of niggling injuries, he played only half of the 1933-34 season, only this time was fit for the repeat trip to Wembley. And how City needed him! Prior to the Final against Portsmouth he'd already scored seven times in the Cup including four in the 6-1 semi-final triumph over Aston Villa. At Wembley the Blues were a goal down at half-time. In the changing rooms a disgruntled Frank Swift was apologising to all and sundry for not keeping out the Portsmouth goal. In his broad Barnsley tones, Tilson consoled the young goalkeeper by telling him, "Tha don't need to worry – I'll plonk in tow in t' next 'arf." The confident Yorkshireman was true to his word and the Cup came back to Manchester for the first time in 30 years. That same summer he was capped by England for the first time. Just to prove that the opposition made no difference to him, he scored six times in his four international appearances.

Not surprisingly by now Tilson was a firm favourite with the supporters as well as being an integral part of a very formidable City side. In 1937 they were crowned First Division champions and although both Brook and Doherty had eclipsed him in the goalscoring stakes, his 15 goals were a critical part of that success. In the space of three days in February he scored two hat-tricks in successive games, against Derby and Wolves. At nearly 34 years of age it seemed as though he'd lost little of his sharpness in front of goal.

Despite his advancing years many City fans were sad to see Tilson leave the club in March 1938 after 10 years loyal service. He was transferred to Northampton Town but returned to Maine Road a few years later in a variety of backroom jobs and was even there during Joe Mercer and Malcolm Allison's time, right up until his retirement in 1967.

With a goal almost every other game, Tilson's achievements have been beaten only by seven men in the club's history. Ironically the man in top spot is his old Barnsley pal Eric Brook. Had he had better luck with regard to his fitness it seems likely that he would have been even higher in that most impressive list.

Following a short illness, Freddie Tilson died in November 1972, aged 69.

Maine Road career

275 appearances   132 goals

Ernie Toseland – model of consistency

OUTSIDE-RIGHT Ernie Toseland was one of the most permanent features in City sides of the 1930s, one of the strongest periods in the club's history.

He joined the Blues in March 1929 from Coventry where he'd already made a name for himself with 11 goals in just 22 starts for the Midlanders. He played in three games (the last three) of the 1928-29 season – scoring once, in his second game, a 3-0 win against Aston Villa. For the next nine years he averaged slightly more than 38 League games a season; a remarkable achievement over such a long period of time. Remember too these were the days of 42 League games a season.

At Maine Road, Toseland's number one priority was to provide the service for Messrs. Tilson, Brook, Herd and later Doherty, the prolific strike force for the Blues at the time. This he managed without fail week after week, performances that would have won him a host of international caps had it done been for an excess of exceptional English wingers around at the same time. The nearest he got to international recognition was a solitary game for the Football League against the Irish League in September 1929.

Born in Kettering in March 1905, Toseland had been a rugby three-quarter in his younger days, a position and sport that no doubt helped to increase his speed and stamina, both qualities he had ample supplies of during his days with City.

As already mentioned, Toseland was not expected to be a major goalscorer for the Blues although on occasion he seemed to forget the fact and reverted back to his earlier ways at Coventry. In four out of six seasons he netted double figures (a more than acceptable return for a winger) and scored in successive FA Cup semi-finals, in 1933 and 1934.

He was an ever present in the successful championship winning season of 1936-37, a feat he'd already achieved twice before. His winners' medal now took pride of place in the Toseland household alongside his FA Cup winners' one from 1934.

Toseland could be compared to Neil Young as a player with Manchester City. Admittedly their styles differed immeasurably but they were both crucial members of highly successful sides (both won the FA Cup and the championship) who tended to get overlooked at the expense of the more glamourous 'star' players. In Young's case it was Lee, Bell and Summerbee. Perhaps in Toseland's case it was Swift, Brook and Doherty. And yet both men played more than 400 times for the Blues, indicative of their level of consistency and the high esteem their respective managers held them in. Toseland and Young were equally highly thought of by two sets of teammates and fans a generation apart. Even the seemingly remote City Board of Directors valued Toseland's efforts; they offered him a £650 benefit as a token of their appreciation.

Midway through the 1938-39 season the 34-year-old Toseland joined Sheffield Wednesday where he managed just 15 games before the outbreak of World War Two forced his premature retirement. He guested for City twice during the war and continued playing into his 40s in the Cheshire County League.

Ernie Toseland is a largely forgotten man in the annals of Manchester City Football Club, a great shame when people look closely at his achievements and length of time spent at Maine Road. Many players who've contributed considerably less to the cause are remembered much more fondly, and easily. It is hoped that by mentioning him in this book of legends, his contribution will be given greater consideration.

He passed away in October 1987, aged 82.

Maine Road career

411 appearances   75 goals

Bert Trautmann – steppes to Wembley

WITHOUT doubt one of the finest goalkeepers the game has ever seen, Bert Trautmann is not only a footballing legend in his adopted Manchester but all over the world. His whole life, let alone his footballing career, reads like an adventure story and would make for compulsive viewing should it ever be filmed.

Bernhard Carl Trautmann was born in Bremen on 23 October 1923 and curiously enough with what he'd become in later life, was actually a schoolboy centre-forward. His working life began as an apprentice motor mechanic, a trade he completed before joining the Luftwaffe in 1941 as a wireless operator. He saw active service in Poland and Russia (where he nearly died because of the intense cold), later becoming a paratrooper, one who would win medals for bravery. After being caught on two previous occasions (and escaping both times) Trautmann was finally captured by the Americans in Normandy and then shipped to a prisoner-of-war camp at Ashton-in-Makerfield in Lancashire. It was at this camp that, owing to injury, he tried his hand in goal in one of the makeshift football games. It was the first step in a remarkable goalkeeping career.

After the war he stayed in Lancashire and began playing in goal for St Helens Town; that is of course when time off from bomb disposal duties would allow. In 1949 City were looking for a replacement for Frank Swift and news reached manager Jock Thomson of the abilities of a strapping German currently playing amateur football on Merseyside. On 7 October that year Trautmann signed amateur forms for the Blues. He was so good even then that within a month he'd turned professional with a £550 price tag. The war was still fresh in the minds of the Manchester public and the thought of City paying money for and to a former German paratrooper angered many of them. The club received a series of hostile letters and threats, many even suggesting they were going to burn their season tickets and never set foot near Maine Road again. Fortunately the players felt differently. They were only concerned in what Trautmann could do in the future, not what he'd done in the past and to a man they helped him quickly settle in during what was the trickiest of times.

Trautmann soon realised that the best way to win over the fans was to prove himself on the pitch. Even though his debut started badly (City lost 3-0 at Bolton) fans soon realise that no matter what colour or creed a man is, when he's got a City jersey on he's 'one of us'. Especially when the 'one of us' is the main difference between a win and a defeat. In many instances Trautmann was the difference between a defeat and a mauling!

For six seasons from 1950-51 onwards Trautmann missed a total of five League games. For three of those seasons he was an ever-present. This remarkable run was only interrupted by the events of the 1956 FA Cup Final, when, as has been much chronicled in the past, he amazingly continued to play on in goal despite suffering a broken neck. Despite the severity of his injury, Trautmann was back in goal for the Blues seven months later.

1956 was a year of mixed fortunes for this great goalkeeper. As well as being on the winning side in the FA Cup Final he also won the Footballer of the Year Award. On the dark side of course was his injury and, even worse, the tragic loss of his young son in a traffic accident.

When he finally retired eight years later, he'd played 545 times in 15 seasons for City, an appearance record bettered only by three other players. An official crowd of 48,000 watched his testimonial game on 15 April 1964 although it is felt that many more did not pay to gain admission whilst thousands simply could not get in at all. Perhaps the biggest disappointment in Trautmann's career was the fact that politics prevented him from playing for his country. Because of where he earned his living, the German authorities simply refused to let him play international football, the nearest he came was playing twice for the Football League.

After a few games with Wellington Town, Trautmann became manager at Stockport County, taking time out occasionally to do some PR work for Simpson's Hazel Grove based meat-processing company. He later became a much sought after coach, travelling all over the world, staying for long periods in the Far East and Africa.

In recent times he has settled down to enjoy his retirement in Spain but does try to make a rare, but nevertheless welcome, visit to Manchester once every couple of years. When he officially opened the new Kippax Street Stand in 1995 he received a hero's reception, an indication of the affection he is still held in by City fans more than 30 years after he last played for them. Bert Trautmann was quite simply a magnificent goalkeeper. There is nothing else to be said.

Maine Road career
545 appearances

Dennis Tueart – skilful, pacey, direct

DENNIS Tueart scored one of the most important goals in Manchester City's history as well as one of the most spectacular ever seen at Wembley.

The game was the 1976 Football League Cup Final when Tueart's marvellously athletic overhead kick proved to be the decisive goal and win for City what was, until the end of the 2001-02 season, their last piece of silverware. Now a director at Maine Road, no one more that Tueart himself will be delighted that his particular achievement has finally been eclipsed.

He'd been a Wembley winner prior to that game against Newcastle, when he played for Second Division Sunderland in their surprise victory against Don Revie's all-conquering Leeds United in the 1973 FA Cup Final. Born in Newcastle in November 1949, Sunderland had been Tueart's first club, having joined them as a junior in August 1967. Once established in the first team at Roker Park, he scored nearly fifty goals in 173 League games before a move to Maine Road in March 1974.

Tueart was a joint signing with Micky Horswill (a deal that saw Tony Towers move to the north-east) and both made their debuts 48 hours later in the heat of a Manchester 'derby'. It was a 'derby' hotter than most with Mike Doyle and United's Lou Macari being sent off and referee Clive Thomas taking both sets of players off the pitch for a cooling off period. The ensuing goalless draw proved to be the biggest disappointment of the afternoon. By the time his next game against United came around, City were in a position of mid-table security whereas United desperately needed the points to stave off relegation. Denis Law's goal for City proved to be enough to settle the outcome shortly before an abortive pitch invasion by the devastated Reds' fans. In two months Dennis Tueart had discovered just what playing football in Manchester was all about.

For the next four years he played a crucial role in a City side that featured regularly at the top of Division One. He top scored with 24 goals in the 1975-76 season and finished runner-up in the other three. He also became the regular penalty-taker; with 24 successful conversions (in both spells) only Francis Lee and Eric Brook have scored more. Not surprisingly, Dennis Tueart was a tremendously popular figure on the terraces. When he got the ball fans knew he only had one idea in mind.

In February 1978 he decided to try his luck in the then buoyant surroundings of the NASL and joined the star-studded New York Cosmos for £250,000. Just short of two years later he was back in Moss Side. Like his first debut, his second (against Norwich) on 1 March 1980 was also goalless. As opposed to many leaving Maine Road under Malcolm Allison's second reign, Tueart was one of the ones actually brought in; curiously his appearances became less under Allison's replacement John Bond. Had Tueart not broken a wrist causing him to miss five crucial League games in September and October 1980 perhaps Allison's departure wouldn't have been as swift.

He left Maine Road again at the end of the 1982-83 season, his last game in City's colours coming in the tragic 1-0 home defeat by Luton Town, a result that saw the Blues relegated and the visitors survive. He even admits to a 'confrontation' with Luton's Brian Horton immediately after the final whistle such was his frustration and disappointment.

He'd played more than 250 times for City (as well as six times for England, his complete tally) and left following the worst circumstances imaginable. After City, Tueart joined Stoke for just two games before finishing his career with Burnley. Following his retirement from the game he opened his own travel firm in Cheadle and then later a sports hospitality and management company. At the time of writing he is on the board of directors at Maine Road (having joined in 1997) with special responsibilities for 'all footballing matters'. He was a key figure in bringing Kevin Keegan to City in the summer of 2001 so he appears to be doing his new job just as well and with as much enthusiasm as he did his old one!

Maine Road career
265-10 appearances   109 goals

Dave Watson – truly a rock

ENGLAND centre-half Dave Watson paraded the League Cup around Wembley in 1976 with blood oozing from a cut just above his left eye and a not inconsiderable amount of the same substance adorning his sky-blue shirt. In the changing room shortly after the game, television cameras showed the wound being stitched as Watson happily chatted away to the interviewer. It was obviously a painful experience, one that made even those watching flinch, and yet it only confirmed the bravery and courage of one of City's finest ever defenders. The only person not troubled by the injury was Watson himself. He appeared to shrug the whole thing off as nothing more than a slight shaving mishap. City fans of that era (and opposition forwards) knew only too well just how tough 'Big Dave' was.

The words 'hard' and 'dirty' are sometimes confused, especially when used to describe strapping six-foot plus central defenders. Only one of these could be used fairly to describe Watson correctly; it is most certainly not the second one. There was no questioning his solidity. There was also no questioning his honesty and heading ability. It seemed sometimes that Watson's headed clearances went further than his teammates kicked ones.

Watson was born in Stapleford in 1947 and began his playing career as a 20-year-old centre-forward with Notts County. Twelve months later he joined Tommy Docherty's Rotherham United but it was a £100,000 move to Sunderland in December 1970 that really got his career going. Under Bob Stokoe, Sunderland became of the strongest teams outside of the top division. Playing alongside the likes of goalkeeper Jimmy Montgomery and centre-forward Billy Hughes (not to mention Dennis Tueart on the wing) Sunderland proved to be a surprise package in the 1973 FA Cup when they defeated the mighty Leeds United thanks to Ian Porterfield's goal at Wembley. Still with the Second Division outfit the following summer, he was rewarded with the first of his 65 England caps (three as captain) when he replaced Roy McFarland in the goalless draw with Portugal in Lisbon.

On 13 June 1975 Tony Book secured his services for City on a six-year contract worth £275,000 and involving City's Jeff Clarke. It was undoubtedly money well spent. Seldom has a player either before or since, showed such battling qualities as Watson possessed. His debut came in the opening game of the 1975-76 season, a 3-0 win at Norwich, a season that culminated in that League Cup triumph against Newcastle. He was a virtual ever-present for the following two seasons (he missed just one League game in each campaign) collecting City's Player of the Year trophy in 1977, a few weeks after the Blues had missed out on the First Division title by one point to Liverpool.

By this time he had firmly established himself as England's first choice centre-half. Such was his resolve to play for both club and country that on more than one occasion he played when less than 100% fit, shrugging off without a second glance a series of irritating injuries that would have sidelined many players with less determination for a fight. Well aware of these strengths, Tony Book rewarded him with the captaincy for the start of the 1977-78 season, taking over from another player cut from the same cloth, Mike Doyle.

Like many others, Watson found himself a victim of Malcolm Allison's apparently all-sweeping new broom and moved to German side FC Werder Bremen in June 1979. He spent a fairly unhappy few months in Germany before returning to England and Southampton. His two years at The Dell he proved he'd lost none of his sharpness, winning a further 18 caps to go with the 30 he won whilst in City's colours. Only Colin Bell has won more as a City player.

In the early 1980s he played for Stoke City, Derby and Notts County, creating a new international record at Stoke in 1982 when he was capped for England with his fifth different club. Vancouver Whitecaps and Fort Lauderdale Strikers also benefited from Watson's experience before he finally hung his boots up after a time with non-Leaguers Kettering Town.

Watson played less than 200 times for City but was still playing football six years after he left Maine Road. Had he stayed, it seems perfectly plausible that the lean years immediately following his departure would not have been so. There have been many times in the 23 years since when City fans have been heard to say, "Oh, I wish we had another Dave Watson." Regretably his kind don't come along too often.

Maine Road career

188 appearances   6 goals

Nicky Weaver – the best is yet to come

GOALKEEPER Nicky Weaver joined City in May 1997 from Mansfield Town on the recommendation of then goalkeeping coach Alex Stepney. The former Manchester United and England goalkeeper was quoted at the time as saying the 6ft 3ins, 18-year-old Weaver was already "worth £16 million." Fortunately he only cost the Blues £100,000 and it has certainly been money well spent.

Taking over from Martyn Margetson and Tommy Wright (both of whom had been the number one choice the previous season), Weaver came into the first team for the opening game of the 1998-99 season. When it finished 10 months later, he'd played in a remarkable 55 matches, more than any other individual. Following an impressive debut in a 3-0 win against Blackpool, Weaver missed just three games all season and showed not only tremendous ability but also remarkable confidence in one so young. It was this confidence between the posts that permeated its way throughout the entire defence, culminating in the pulsating Second Division play-off Final against Gillingham at Wembley. Having been beaten twice during normal play, Weaver then saved twice during the ensuing penalty shoot out before setting off on a celebratory frenzied sprint around the famous old stadium.

A major factor in City's successful promotion had been down to the fact that they'd conceded just 33 times in the League, only one more than champions Fulham. On Weaver's part, he'd kept a clean sheet on a total of 24 occasions, a new club record, beating Alex Williams' one of 14 years earlier.

He continued his fine performances throughout the following season, one that again resulted in promotion. For the second consecutive season Weaver's contribution was a huge one. He missed just one game through a bout of 'flu and City's record of 40 goals conceded was the best in the Division. It was this consistent run of good form that brought him to the attention of the England selectors and he was capped at Under-21 level and played in that age group's European championships in the summer of 2000. What should be noted here is the contribution the Blues' second-choice goalkeeper Tommy Wright made to Weaver's blossoming career. A vastly experienced and talented goalkeeper in his own right, the Northern Ireland international could easily have moved on to another club but preferred instead to stay at Maine Road and contribute to Weaver's development.

By the time City began their Premiership campaign in August that year, Weaver was still only 21 and already a 'veteran' of more than 100 first-team games. With a better quality of strikers facing them, the Sheffield-born goalkeeper and his erstwhile defensive teammates found life somewhat harder than they'd been used to. Mistakes made in the lower divisions often went unpunished but it proved to be a different kettle of fish now City were in amongst 'the big boys'. For most of the season the Blues struggled and would eventually suffer relegation. Weaver was not the only one to make some glaring errors, the result of which caused concerns about his ability to compete at the highest level as well as knocking his hitherto supreme confidence. Consequently his form suffered, Carlo Nash came in from nearby Stockport County and Weaver lost his position in the side.

But Weaver is certainly not a loser and began to work harder in training, lost some weight and changed his lifestyle and was back vying for top spot with Nash in August 2001. There is little to chose between the two 'keepers and the Blues are very fortunate to have two men of such high standards to call on. Both are big, strong, powerful men who are particularly good shot stoppers not afraid to throw themselves into the thickest of the action. Appearances-wise, Weaver had a slight edge until a knee injury sustained at Birmingham in March 2002 handed the job to Nash for the rest of the successful championship season.

Just days after clinching the First Division championship in April, Kevin Keegan acquired the services of the legendary Danish goalkeeper Peter Schmeichel from Aston Villa. At 38 (and as with Stuart Pearce) it appears to be a one-season deal although stories already suggest that the former Manchester United player will go straight into the first team. Rather than treating it as a threat, Weaver saw Schmeichel's arrival as a massive benefit for the club as a whole and for him in particular saying he couldn't wait to work alongside him and undoubtedly learn from one of the best in the world.

Remarkably only 23, Nicky Weaver is still some 10 years from being in his prime as a goalkeeper. Don't for one minute rule out his chances of once again of becoming City's number one, or for that matter, England's.

Maine Road career
178-1 appearances   (to the end of the 2001-02 season)

Eric Westwood – a man for all seasons

MANCHESTER-BORN full-back Eric Westwood is one of a relatively small number of footballers who've been on the books of both Manchester clubs. He is also one of an even more select bunch of players, those who played for the same team in three different decades.

I had the privilege of interviewing Westwood back in the summer of 1998 for an article in the club's monthly magazine. Even though he was just a couple of months away from his 81st birthday he was still a powerful, craggy looking man, one who still had an opinion or two about the game as well as a razor-sharp memory. Looking at photographs of him in his prime suggest that as a player he was taught in the 'take no prisoners' school of defenders. Wingers who tried their luck against him would have known they'd been in a game as Saturday evenings wore on. The phrase 'hard but fair' could have been penned originally for Eric Westwood. For all his appearance and no-nonsense tackling, Westwood was booked just once during his City career, and that was for swearing at Roy Clarke!

He'd originally joined United as an amateur after impressing scouts in schoolboy games. As a young teenager he was in the Manchester Boys side that played against Southampton Boys in a two-legged English Shield Final, the home leg being played at Maine Road. In front of 40,000 people Westwood scored in the drawn game. As a registered player with the Blues for nearly 16 years, he rated this as his single most outstanding memory.

Frank Swift predicted Westwood's debut even before the player himself had been notified. Travelling back to Manchester on the coach from a reserve team game at Derby (amazingly Swift had been dropped from the first team) news got through to the players that the senior side had lost 6-1 to Millwall at Maine Road. Swift turned to Westwood and said, "You'll be in the first team soon." Six games later Swift's prophecy came true. Westwood made his debut against Tottenham in a 2-0 on 5 November 1938, the same game as Bert Sproston's debut. The day before Sproston had himself been a Spurs' player and had signed for the Blues on the Friday night. It was the beginning of a marvellous full-back pairing for the club.

Westwood never missed a League game until World War Two interrupted football in September 1939, 33 games later. After being called up for service in January 1940 he stayed in the army for six and a half years. During the war he played 23 times for the Blues, guested for Reading, Norwich and Chelsea and even played for the Londoners in the 1944 FA War Cup Final at Wembley. He was posted to Normandy shortly after D-Day and at the end of the war was close to the advancing Russians in Germany. He was still only 27 and was awarded the captaincy of the British Army on the Rhine team that travelled all over Europe playing a series of competitive friendlies.

When he came back to City in the 1946-47 season he was unable to regain his regular position at left-back owing to the continuing good form of his replacement Sam Barkas. Instead he had to settle for a place on the left-wing, a position he held until the summer of 1947 when captain Barkas moved on to Workington. By his own admission he was quite happy playing out wide, and was equally happy when he collected a Second Division championship medal at the end of his first season back.

With Barkas moving on, manager Jock Thomson was in need of an experienced player to take over the captains' responsibilities and Westwood fitted the bill perfectly. He was captain for the next four years, a period that coincided with Bert Trautmann's arrival and one in which Westwood was harshly treated by some supporters for his supposed sole responsibility for signing 'the dreaded German'.

In June 1953, the Football League representative and England B player was given a free transfer and joined non-League Altrincham on a part-time basis in order to give him time to run the Talbot pub in Stretford. He later had his own newsagents on Mauldeth Road before retiring in 1975.

When he left Maine Road he was summoned to the boardroom and given a cheque for £750 gross, £412 net. Football has certainly come a long way since Eric Westwood stopped playing. In the summer of 2001, just a few weeks before City's successful Championship campaign began, he passed away aged 83.

Maine Road career

260 appearances   5 goals   (not including wartime appearances)

David White – supplier and scorer

IN the late 1980s and early 1990s, there was no finer sight at Maine Road than a rampaging David White running full speed at back-pedalling opposition defences. Apart from his happy knack of scoring the more than occasional goal and his ability to provide great crosses for Niall Quinn, another reason for his popularity amongst supporters was that he was one of them.

Urmston born and a former Salford Lads' player, White signed apprentice forms for City on his 18th birthday – 30 October 1985 – and was yet another product of the successful FA Youth Cup winning side of 1986.

On 27 September that year he made his first senior appearance when he came on as a replacement for the injured Trevor Christie in a 1-0 defeat at Luton. It was a season of mixed fortunes for White. He played some part in 30 games that season, a difficult one for the most part and one that ultimately ended in relegation. His only goal that campaign came in a 3-1 home win against West Ham in December. Having once established himself in the senior side he became a regular starter for new manager Mel Machin in the Blues' attempt to regain promotion. Against Huddersfield Town in November 1987, White was one of three players (Paul Stewart and Tony Adcock being the others) who scored a hat-trick in the 10-1 massacre.

Promotion was achieved after two years at Bradford in May 1989. Including Cup ties, White played in 50/1 games, scoring eight times and it was his cross to Trevor Morley with just four minutes to go at Bradford that provided City with the vital point needed to clinch second place.

Back in the top flight, White continued his fine performances (not least in the 5-1 game against Manchester United) and shared the top goalscoring spot with Clive Allen with 11 strikes each. The arrival of Niall Quinn in March 1990 took White's career on even further with the big Irishman providing both a target and a perfect foil as the productive partnership between them produced 39 goals. White's personal contribution of 17 included four at Villa Park as City cantered to another 5-1 victory.

With the Blues now under Peter Reid's charge, they enjoyed two consecutive fifth place positions in the last two years before the introduction of the Premiership. These were indeed heady days at Maine Road, the positions being the best since Tony Book's side in 1978. David White was a major factor in the Blues' resurgence during this period. His pace always caused problems for defenders and a hat-trick at Oldham on the last day of the 1991-92 season took his goals tally in all competitions to 21, his best ever return. It was this continuing run of good form that brought him to the attention of the England selectors.

In September 1992 he won his one and only full international cap when he played against Spain in Santander. England lost the game 1-0 with White having the misfortune to miss a clear-cut chance (one he would normally have put away easily in a City shirt) with his first kick of the game. The miss proved costly not only in the context of the game but also in its aftermath with many people apportioning the blame squarely on the City player's shoulders. The experience undoubtedly affected his confidence and perhaps with a little less criticism – and another chance – he might have gone on to win more caps.

Back at Maine Road, he was an ever-present in the inaugural Premier League season and his goal against Queens Park Rangers on the opening day will forever guarantee him a place in the history books as it was the club's first in the new League.

By December 1993 it appeared as though White was suffering from a lack of confidence and consequently his form suffered. Three days before Christmas he moved to Leeds United in an exchange deal for David Rocastle valued at £1.2 million. There seemed no one particular reason for White's loss of form although some put it down to the disappointment with England over a year since. After Leeds he again teamed up with Howard Kendall, this time at Sheffield United, but a series of niggling injuries brought about an early retirement in 1997.

In recent times, White has provided expert analysis on City games for local radio as well as setting up his own soccer schools. Still recognised and popular with City supporters, White's fast and direct style of play won him many plaudits during his seven years with the club.

Maine Road career
328-14 appearances   95 goals

Wilf Wild – 30 years of loyalty and devotion

FROM March 1932 to November 1946 Wilf Wild was the manager of Manchester City. His 14-year reign make him City's longest serving manager to date. In these days of managerial merry-go-rounds (of which the Blues have been victims of seemingly far too much for their own good) it would indicate that Wild's record will be safe for a while yet.

And yet Wild wasn't just the manager at Maine Road. He'd began as assistant secretary in 1920 working under Ernest Mangnall, then progressed to secretary four years later. He'd always been an advocate of the manager being solely responsible for team matters, leaving all the administrative tasks to behind-the-scenes staff such as himself. In 1932 though he found himself having to perform both posts when previous manager Peter Hodge moved back to Leicester.

His first two years in charge saw City reach Wembley twice. The first occasion in 1933, the Blues had to settle for runners-up medals after a 3-0 defeat by Everton. 12 months later they'd come back from a goal behind to clinch victory over Portsmouth. Wild presided over a fine City side, one that contained some of the country's best players and was watched regularly by crowds averaging well in excess of 30,000 for games at Maine Road. A record crowd of 84,569 watched the game against Stoke in the sixth round of the FA Cup in 1934. No doubt manager Wild was delighted by the 1-0 win, but (with his secretary's head on as well) must have been equally delighted by the gate receipts of nearly £5,500.

It was also under Wild's stewardship that the Blues won – for the very first time – the ultimate prize, the Division One championship, in 1937. That 1936-37 season could have finished so differently. By Christmas, City had only managed to acquire 20 points; nowhere near enough to suggest anything more than mid-table security would be assured. The New Year though marked a sharp contrast. With Doherty especially in marvellous goalscoring form, City embarked on an unbeaten run of 20 games (16 wins and 4 draws) to win the title by three clear points from second placed Charlton. During that run Derby and Liverpool were both beaten 5-0 whilst Bolton went exactly the same way in the FA Cup.

By a remarkable turn of events – and with largely the same team – Wild's side (the division's top scorers) were relegated 12 months later. There seemed little reason why players of the calibre of Swift, Brook and Westwood would have to earn their living in the Second Division, and yet, thanks to World War Two, that's more or less what they'd have to do until the return of League football in August 1946.

As with Mangnall 20 years before, Wild had the less than envious task of keeping the club afloat during the rigours of war. Whereas Mangnall's Hyde Road ground was used as stables, Wild's Maine Road was used for military storage of a whole manner of things, most of which only got in the way of the more mundane matters of stadium and pitch maintenance. It no doubt put Wild under considerable stress and after three months of the first season back after the war, he (possibly willingly) handed over the manager's reigns to former captain Sam Cowan. The no doubt relieved Wild slipped back quietly into his former role as secretary. Ironically City would be crowned Second Division champions at the end of that season.

He remained as club secretary right up until his death in December 1950, a loss that ended 30 years of loyal and devoted service to the club. His wife Betty proved equally as loyal to City, working in the club offices for more than 10 years after her husband's death.

As manager of Manchester City, Wilf Wild won more trophies than any of the eight men who'd held the position previously. It is a record he was quite rightly very proud of.

Alex Williams MBE – still in safe hands

YOU would have to go a long way to find someone as cheerful and affable as the former City goalkeeper Alex Williams. Even on a bleak winter's morning, when fans are huddled together to shelter from the wind and rain as they queue for next week's match tickets, Alex Williams always seems to be around, always with a smile on his face and a cheery "OK?" and a thumbs up for everyone whether he knows them or not. As a representative for the club you would struggle to find someone better and as the club's Football in the Community manager he is in the perfect job.

Born in Moss Side on 13 November 1961, Williams' love affair with City began as a supporter standing on the Kippax. By the time he was 16 he was the first choice goalkeeper for Manchester Boys and had been on the books at Maine Road for almost two years. Like many other aspiring footballers though, Williams, by his own account, thought that his career was going nowhere until one day, out of the blue, Steve Fleet offered him an apprenticeship place. The date was 11 July 1978 and it took Williams less than a second to make up his mind.

After progressing through both the youth and reserve sides, Williams' big chance in the first team came on 14 March 1981 in a 2-1 win against West Bromwich Albion at Maine Road. Had it not been for Bryan Robson's header shortly before the end, it would have been the first of many clean sheets the more than competent goalkeeper would keep in his career. Ironically enough that same player scored in Williams' last game for the Blues as well; this time in the colours of Manchester United, a penalty in their 3-0 win at Maine Road in September 1985.

Only the small matter of Joe Corrigan stood in the way of William's progress and he would have to wait until March 1983 when the giant England goalkeeper moved to Seattle Sounders of the NASL before finally taking over the number one spot. Corrigan was quoted at the time as saying he had every confidence in his successor and so it proved. After just 12 opportunities in the previous two years, Williams began an unbroken run of 94 League appearances that would take him through to the start of the 1985-86 season. A steady, no frills goalkeeper, he had the misfortune of being in goal in the infamous relegation game against Luton in 1983 but then played a key part in the promotion campaign two years later when his 21 clean sheets in the League established a new club record.

A black goalkeeper in the 1980s was somewhat of a novelty in England and Williams suffered some terrible abuse at the hands of supporters of clubs who should most certainly have known differently. Amazingly it did not seem to bother him (at least outwardly) and no doubt he filed all this abuse away mentally, recounting its obvious negatives years later in his job working with schoolchildren.

Playing for the reserves in September 1985, Williams injured his back but did not realise the seriousness of the injury. Desperate to continue his run in the first team – and well aware of Eric Nixon waiting in the wings – he carried on playing until the pain became unbearable and a slipped disc was diagnosed and eventually surgically removed. It marked the end of his Maine Road playing days although he did spend a short while at Queen of the South on loan before finishing his career after 35 League games for Port Vale in 1989.

It was at Port Vale that he first became involved in the Football in the Community programme. Two years later he was offered a similar post back at Maine Road. Even though he thoroughly enjoyed his time in the Potteries, Williams was delighted to come home.

Over the ensuing 11 years much praise has been heaped on City's Football in the Community Programme from a wide variety of sources and a great deal of the credit for that must surely go to Alex Williams. His responsibilities include anything from getting kids involved in football right the way through to education and a whole range of social awareness problems. His team of 20 speaks to approximately 85,000 schoolchildren every year, a monumental exercise in organisation alone even before the education side of things comes in.

After being proposed initially by Mike Summerbee, Alex Williams was awarded the MBE in the 2002 New Years' Honours list. The honour could not have been bestowed on a more worthy recipient.

Maine Road career

125 appearances

Max Woosnam – gentleman footballer

MAX Woosnam was undoubtedly one of the most accomplished all-round sportsmen of the Edwardian era, although when looking at his achievements overall it could be said he was one of the greatest sportsmen of any era.

Born in Liverpool on 6 September 1892, the son of a former Canon of Chester excelled not only at football, but also at tennis, cricket and golf. Initially a student at Winchester, Woosnam moved to Trinity College, Cambridge, where he won his Blue at soccer, golf and tennis, failing initially by the shortest of margins at cricket where he could only make the twelfth man spot. He made up for it after the war when he returned as captain of the First XI.

Apart from his success on the football field with City, Woosnam's other greatest sporting achievements came on the tennis courts. Along with doubles partner Noel Turnbull he won the gold medal at the 1920 Olympics in Antwerp, a tournament that saw the five rings symbol used for the very first time. That same year he was also in the winning doubles team in the Davis Cup whilst in 1921 with a new partner, Australian Randolph Lycett, he became Wimbledon doubles champion. For good measure he was runner-up in the mixed doubles final (with Miss P.L.Howkins) that same year.

On the footballing side, centre-half Woosnam had played for Corinthians and was on tour with them in Brazil when war broke out in 1914. On his return to England he joined the Montgomeryshire Yeomanry before later being transferred to the Royal Welch Fusiliers. Woosnam was no doubt perfect officer material and had the necessary good looks to go with it. With his immaculately centre-parted hair and neatly clipped curly moustache he epitomised an Edwardian gentleman. In simple terms, he looked like one of the Bellamy family in television's *Upstairs, Downstairs*.

His flawless appearance never altered when it came to playing football either. The staunch amateur player was often seen jogging around the pitch still holding a silk handkerchief. In addition to Corinithians, Woosnam had also represented Chelsea before arriving at Hyde Road in November 1919, quite what the flat-capped Mancunians thought when they first caught sight of this 'toff' is unknown but it does seem fair to assume that they'd not seen too many of his kind before, especially on a football field.

No doubt helped by his experiences in the army, Woosnam quickly accustomed himself to the Hyde Road players and fans. He became very popular very quickly and a string of consistently cultured performances in defence earned him his one and only England cap against Wales in 1922. These performances were also enough to promote him to captain, a position he had the honour of holding for the inaugural match at Maine Road in August 1923.

In the last game of the 1921-22 season Woosnam suffered a broken leg after a touchline collision with Lowe of Newcastle. Forever the gentleman he immediately relinquished any blame from Lowe saying, "It was entirely my own fault." Later, on the stretcher going into the back of the waiting ambulance, Woosnam was reported to have asked the stretcher bearers to stop for a moment whilst he signed a young boy's autograph book. What price that kind of behaviour today?

The break proved to be so bad that he missed the entire 1922-23 season, coming back (still heavily strapped below the knee) for that first game at Maine Road 15 months later. The game against Sheffield United was his one and only League appearance that season and he made just two in the following. The injury had effectively curtailed his footballing career prematurely; at barely 30 years of age it was felt he could have carried on for at least a couple of more seasons.

In October 1925 he tried his hand for a while with Northwich Victoria before returning to tennis and became a member of the Northern Lawn Tennis Club in Didsbury. Away from sport he later joined the Northwich firm Brunner Mond, a company that would eventually be bought by ICI. In 1940 Woosnam moved to London when he was offered a position on that company's board of directors, becoming personnel manager until his retirement in 1954.

A man who'd missed games for City whilst away on Davis Cup duty for Britain, passed away in Westminster on 14 July 1965, aged 72.

Hyde Road-Maine Road career

93 appearances   4 goals

Neil Young – the sweetest of left feet

NOT only was Neil Young one of the most graceful players ever to have played for Manchester City but his powerful left-foot was also responsible for scoring some of the most crucial goals in its entire history.

It was his goal that won the 1969 FA Cup Final. He scored the first goal (and was then brought down as he was about to score the second) in the European Cup-winners' Cup Final 12 months later. In the semi-final of that same competition he found the net twice against German side FC Schalke 04. Prior to those goals he'd scored a brace at Newcastle in the championship decider. For a Fallowfield-born City fan who'd stood on the terraces as a teenager in the 1950s, surely such achievements were even beyond the most fertile of dreams and imaginations.

People who knew of City during the great days of the late 1960s and early 1970s but could not be classed as fans, understandably knew the names Lee, Bell and Summerbee, but surprisingly little else. Fans who saw the Blues regularly and even the players themselves knew Neil Young's name should be mentioned in the same breath. Even Mike Summerbee once commented, "They should have named that video Lee, Bell, Summerbee and Young," such was Young's contribution and importance to the side.

He was born in February 1944 and after playing for school and Manchester Boys he signed for City as an amateur three months after his 15th birthday. He had to wait more than two years later for his first team debut, a 2-1 defeat at Aston Villa in November 1961. In his early days he was tried out as both a right and left-winger as well as the occasional centre-forward but the arrival of Mercer and Allison in the summer of 1965 transformed him not only into an inside-left of the highest quality but also a prolific goalscorer. He topped scored in City's Second Division championship season of 1965-66 and then again in the First Division triumph two years later.

For the best part of six years he was an integral part of an all-conquering City side. A tall, slim figure, the sight of Young in full flow then finally releasing a shot on goal truly was one to behold and he was much loved by the fans, after all at the end of the day, he'd been one himself not too long ago. Apart from the fact that he was a very good player, perhaps it was this real 'local boy made good' situation that adhered him to the fans even more. Even though it's been more than 30 years since Young kicked a ball for City his popularity with the fans shows no signs of waning, a fact proved with the huge support he was given during his recent benefit campaign.

In the early part of 1972 Young knew his days were numbered as Malcolm Allison was set on buying Rodney Marsh from Queen's Park Rangers. He also knew that Allison still needed some extra finance and that Marsh would be playing in the number 10 shirt if and when he eventually arrived at Maine Road. Because of that, along with David Connor, Young found himself being sold to Preston North End for a £48,000 fee. The player claims he was promised (he was most certainly due) a testimonial game at the time of the move, a game that unfortunately never materialised and consequently frustrated him. He would stay away from Maine Road until 1994 when his good friend (former teammate and then chairman) Francis Lee invited him back.

After two seasons with Preston, Young finished his playing career with a handful of games at Rochdale in 1974. When his footballing days were over he had a variety of jobs including an insurance salesman, removal man and a milkman but also suffered badly with his health, a bad back and an almost fatal deep vein thrombosis being the most serious complaints.

Not surprisingly the loss of revenue from that never-played testimonial game frustrated Young for many years after his retirement. In 2000 a group of dedicated City supporters decided to try and set the records straight and having obtained the backing of the club and many of Young's former playing colleagues, began a year long round of dinners and other benefit functions.

Currently living in Handforth and running his own soccer schools, it seems a shame that Young and City parted in such a way. Neil Young contributed greatly to the most successful period in City's history and with the Blues now back in the top division again (one that Young graced so successfully) it would be nice to see 'Nelly' back at Maine Road. There is no doubting the reception he'd get from the fans.

Maine Road career

413-3 appearances   108 goals

Bibliography

Cawley, Steve & James Gary *The Pride of Manchester* (ACL Polar, 1991)

Goble, Ray & Ward, Andrew *Manchester City - A Complete Record* (Breedon Books, 1987 & 1993)

Harding, John *Football Wizard - The Story of Billy Meredith* (Breedon Books, 1985)

Hugman, Barry J. ed *The PFA Premier & Football League Players' Records 1946-1998* Queen Anne Press 1998

James, Gary *Manchester: The Greatest City* Polar 1997

Maddocks, John et al *Manchester City – Cup Kings 1956* Over the Moon 1999

Manchester City Football Club *Official Handbooks* Various

Manchester City Football Club Official match programmes Various

Manchester City Football Club *Official monthly magazines* Various

Parker, Joanne ed *Manchester City Centenary Brochure 1894-95-1994-95* Manchester City Football Club, 1995

Penney, Ian *Manchester City – The Mercer-Allison Years* Breedon Books, 2001

Penney, Ian *The Essential History of Manchester City* Headline, 2000

Penney, Ian *The Maine Road Encyclopedia* Mainstream, 1995

Penney, Ian *Blue Heaven: Manchester City's Greatest Games* Mainstream, 1996

Robinson, Michael *Football League Tables 1888-1997* Soccer Books Ltd, 1997

Rollin, Jack *Rothman's Football Yearbooks* (Various)

Smailes, Gordon *The Breedon Book of Football Records 1871-2000* Breedon Books, 2000

Thornton, Eric *Manchester City – Meredith to Mercer and the FA Cup* Robert Hale, 1969

Turner, Dennis & Alex White *The Breedon Book of Football Managers* Breedon Books, 1993

Ward, Andrew *The Manchester City Story* Breedon Books, 1984